...can become a CEO!

To: Alex Malley
From: Roderick West
Date: 15 April, 2014

Subject: ABC 24 Television

Lord Malley,

I was so proud of you this morning. Impeccably dressed and a clean, shaven countenance.

Your best point was the need for innovation — no masking or bridling. What verbs! Truly Spenserian.

But there is a tragic flaw that you are prone to. That is the automatic use of the singular of the verb 'to be', whether the predicate is singular or plural. You fell twice: 'There HAS been mishaps...' and 'THERE'S some promises...' Something to correct yourself and then you could gently chide your fellow conversationalists. Just a thought.

As Janet so shrewdly observed: 'Why didn't Trinity see all this talent at the time?' I think your mind was occupied elsewhere, as it tore down the paddock with those runaway tries.

The next step is Canberra. I mean it.

Yours ever,

Rod

34 years later, Mr West is still telling me to pull my socks up. At least it is now Lord Malley, not Sandy!

Alex.

'Alex Malley brings great enthusiasm, experience and wisdom to the crucial task of understanding what it takes to be the best possible you. An invaluable handbook for anyone seeking to acquire the secrets of all round success.'

—**The Honourable Richard Alston**

'Life's journey is different for every one of us, and clearly Alex has made an extraordinary journey that will help so many young people realise that energy and determination are every bit as important as paper qualifications.'

—**Lord Jeffrey Archer**, author

'Intellect and skill alone will not make you a real leader. The best leaders that I have observed build relationships through a set of principles which mobilises and unleashes the competencies of those around you, as Alex Malley illustrates in this book. If you get that right then you have a chance to succeed.'

—**Don Argus AO, FCPA**, Chairman of Bank of America Merrill Lynch Australia Advisory Board

'*The Naked CEO* is an inspirational how-to guide for young people looking to get ahead in business and in life. It's a practical and motivational toolkit that I believe gives our next generation every opportunity for success. I look forward to seeing how these young entrepreneurs change our world for the better.'

—**Mark Bouris**, Executive Chairman of Yellow Brick Road and host of *The Celebrity Apprentice Australia*

'I have experienced great success and great failure in my professional life. If you have never known failure you can never really know success and this book will help you understand how to make the most of your failures.'

—**John Brogden AM**, CEO, Financial Services Council, and Chairman, Lifeline Australia

'*The Naked CEO* makes the transition from classroom to conference room a little less daunting for every student beginning their career.'

—**S. Bruce Dowton**, Vice-Chancellor, Macquarie University

'Alex's commitment to leadership goes beyond his connection with the younger generation. Our organisation, our brand and our profession have been greatly enhanced because of his energy, passion and drive that inspires not just our current membership but also the future business leaders of tomorrow.'

—**Penny Egan FCPA**, President and Chairman of the Board, CPA Australia

'I encourage you all to heed Alex's sage advice. I know I would have appreciated it at the same point in my career. Indeed, I'll be sharing Alex's book with my three sons! It's the combination of knuckling down to hard work, being observant and respectful, and then taking on new and bigger challenges that really resonates for me. Go well, and as Alex says, enjoy a big life!'

—**Bruce Gosper**, CEO, Austrade

'Alex Malley shares with us in *The Naked CEO* the rich veins of a life of an extraordinary communicator and leader. In an entertaining way he captivates the reader drawing out wonderful lessons for a good life as he extols us to dare to dream, to have confidence, to respect others and to have an ongoing pursuit of the insight of life. We are lucky Alex has taken the time to write this as I know all of us will be the better for his great stories and advice.'

—**David Gonski AC**

'In creating *The Naked CEO* Alex Malley again demonstrates his true leadership qualities. He provides a trail for others for their own ambition; and his willingness to share shows the mark of a real leader.'

—**Ross Greenwood**, business and finance editor, Nine Network Australia, and 2GB's *Money News* program

'True to form, Alex leaves nothing off the table about leadership and the realities of the workplace.'

—**David Gyngell**, CEO Nine Entertainment Co.

'Alex Malley is a leader that I deeply respect. He is deeply committed to a leader's most important responsibility: to impart their experience and insight. I strongly support his intent to pass the lessons he has learned from a lifetime of good and bad experiences. His book is a guide to advise and assist young people to become successfully established in professional life.'

—**Air Chief Marshal (Ret.) Angus Houston AC, AFC**

'*The Naked CEO* is about the pursuit of insight. It reminds us to look deeper, listen harder, reach further and not least of all, to have faith in ourselves. Alex is a true leader and a passionate educator, and everyone—from student to experienced CEO—can take something from the wisdom he shares in these pages.'

—**Chris Jordan**, Commissioner of Taxation,
Australian Taxation Office

'Alex Malley is fascinated by the secrets of leadership and innovation—in the corporation and in the world. His original book will inspire, stimulate and irritate readers, sometimes, remarkably enough, all at the same time. It is the irritation that creates the pearls.'

—**The Hon Michael Kirby AC, CMG**,
Past Justice of the High Court of Australia

'Last year, millions of young people around the world remained unemployed—more than three times the population of Australia. *The Naked CEO* provides a resource for anyone hoping to navigate the difficult transition from the classroom to the "real world". By sharing his unique experiences and insights, Alex provides a platform from which young people can launch their careers, while also helping them plan for the bold near- and far-term actions that will lead to lasting success.'

—**Andrew N. Liveris**, Chairman & CEO,
The Dow Chemical Company

'Living life to the best of our ability is probably everyone's dream. *The Naked CEO* provides many insightful shortcuts in the rush to lead a better life.'

—**Helen McCabe**, Editor-in-Chief,
The Australian Women's Weekly

'Many CEOs have taken a winding road to the top. Not everyone drove a bright-orange Datsun like Alex did but all have been on a journey that has shaped their skills and outlook, and honed their determination. There is plenty of good advice in this book, particularly that you should never underestimate your ability to influence outcomes, achieve success and make the world a better place along the way.'

—**Ian McPhee PSM, FCPA**, Auditor-General for Australia,
Australian National Audit Office

'Alex Malley's book is all about helping young people have the courage to be the best they can. I urge them to get a copy and read it.'

—**Greg Medcraft**, ASIC Chairman

'Alex Malley is one of Australia's great thinkers and contributors to business and corporate governance.'

—**Nyunggai Warren Mundine**, Chairman, Prime Minister's
Indigenous Advisory Council

'Alex Malley has done some extraordinary things and met many amazing people in his life, and through this book he shares insights and advice collected on his life journey. CPA Australia is to be congratulated for the contribution this book will make to improving management and leadership in Australia.'

—**Christine Nixon APM**, former Chief Commissioner
of Victoria Police

'There are many paths to success in life. Alex Malley shares his own story with unusual honesty and insight. An invaluable roadmap for those aspiring to maximise these career potential and leadership talents.'

—**Susan Pascoe AM**, Australian Charities
and Not-for-profits Commission

'*The Naked CEO* is a truly insightful work which holds great value for anyone looking for personal development or inspiration. Alex Malley has created an amazing book through his honesty and passion to teach. His lessons learnt over a lifetime provide a roadmap for those looking for success and a meaningful life. I highly recommend *The Naked CEO*.'

—**Ben Roberts-Smith VC, MG**, Managing Director,
RS Group Australia

'The insights and experiences Alex shares in this book are an honest and very real reflection of leadership and personal development. The tips are practical and easy to apply and this book will fast become a must read guide for young people about to embark on their career. If every person aspired to a "big life", imagine the potential we could unlock not just in ourselves, but in the broader community in which we exist.'

—**Luke Sayers**, CEO, PwC Australia

'Alex's passion for encouraging people to make the most of their life is genuine and infectious. Alex believes that life is just too important to waste time wondering what might happen. The Alex that I know has endless optimism and endless energy. Take the bold step that he urges you to take.'

—**Tim Sheehy FGIA**, Chief Executive,
Governance Institute of Australia Ltd

'I've always been excited to get out of bed and get to work. Alex clearly has the same excitement each day for teaching and supporting others as they progress in their careers.'

—**Curtis Stone**, chef

'I have admired Alex's commitment to helping young people succeed. The Naked CEO website was a great idea and I believe many talented young people benefitted from the lessons contained in it. This book provides many practical ideas that would benefit ambitious young people.'

—**Giam Swiegers**, CEO, Deloitte Australia

'Alex Malley writes with great clarity, honesty and passion about leadership and life. Whether you agree or disagree with his insights, they'll help you better understand your own challenges and opportunities.'

—**The Honourable Lindsay Tanner**

'A recipe book for success in any field, with practical tips that are easily understood, by someone who has put them into effect with astounding results. Every young person with ambition should read this.'

—**Mark Tedeschi AM, QC**

'Alex Malley is an inspiration. The passion he exudes in every facet of his incredible life is a beauty to behold and the examples he sets and qualities he embodies offer lessons to all of us. Alex is a mentor to the leaders of tomorrow—a wise soul with a brilliant mind who is on a dynamic journey.'

—**Richard Wilkins**, network entertainment editor, Nine Network Australia

'This book will inspire a whole new generation of CEOs. A must read for young students entering the workforce and professionals alike.'

—**Gary Wingrove**, CEO, KPMG Australia

'While the young today need to think big and live life with a passion, they also need the tenacity to hold on to their dreams when faced with obstacles. Alex Malley's new book is an encouraging read for those who want their lives to be meaningful and to make a difference.'

—**Philip Yuen FCPA**, CEO, Deloitte Singapore

'Congratulations to Alex for his heartwarming and insightful account of the learning curve he followed and his leadership principles. His remarkable life journey will serve as an inspiration to future leaders.'

—**Datuk Nor Shamsiah Yunus FCPA**, Deputy Governor, Central Bank of Malaysia

ALEX MALLEY

From suspended schoolboy to disruptive CEO

THE NAKED

CEO

The truth you need
to **build a big life**

WILEY

First published in 2015 by John Wiley & Sons Australia, Ltd
42 McDougall St, Milton Qld 4064

Office also in Melbourne

Typeset in 10/12.5 pt Frutiger LT Std

© CPA Australia Ltd 2015

The moral rights of the author have been asserted

National Library of Australia Cataloguing-in-Publication data:

Author:	Malley, Alex, author.
Title:	The Naked CEO: the truth you need to build a big life / Alex Malley.
ISBN:	9780730314592 (pbk.)
	9780730314608 (ebook)
Notes:	Includes index.
Subjects:	Job enrichment.
	Self-actualization (Psychology).
	Quality of life.
	Life span, Productive.
Dewey Number:	658.31423

Cover design: Xou Creative

Cover image, back cover photo and opening page photo (inset):
© CPA Australia Ltd

Inside front cover image and text: © Trinity Grammar School

Back cover photo (inset) and inside front cover photo (inset): © Alex Malley

Opening page text: © Roderick West

Printed in the U.S.A. by Courier Corporation

10 9 8 7 6 5 4 3 2 1

Disclaimer
The material in this publication is of the nature of general comment only, and does not represent professional advice. It is not intended to provide specific guidance for particular circumstances and it should not be relied on as the basis for any decision to take action or not take action on any matter which it covers. Readers should obtain professional advice where appropriate, before making any such decision. To the maximum extent permitted by law, the author and publisher disclaim all responsibility and liability to any person, arising directly or indirectly from any person taking or not taking action based on the information in this publication.

To my mother, who taught me about unconditional love and the power of dreams. My wonderful and loving wife and partner, Rachel, and our beautiful blended clan in time on the planet order—Emma, Amelia, Amelia (we have two), David, Clare, Julia and young Jack. To my sister Moira, her family and my mates who have been my loyal brothers.

CONTENTS

About Alex Malley   *xvii*

Acknowledgements   *xix*

Prologue   *xxi*

Part I: Dare to dream   1

  1 Be yourself   5

  2 Dreams don't happen overnight   13

  3 Mistakes make you smarter and stronger   19

  4 Insights come from everywhere   27

  5 The black box   35

Part II: Create your own universe   43

  6 Study—finish what you start   47

  7 Networking for novices   55

  8 Get LinkedIn   63

  9 Creating a résumé that gets read   71

 10 Succeeding at job interviews   79

Part III: It's all about the people   91

 11 The first day of a new job   95

 12 Establishing a rapport with your colleagues   101

13	Remembering and using people's names	109
14	Team work and poor team performance	115
15	Getting people to say 'yes'	123

Part IV: Be the best person you can be		**131**
16	Getting organised and getting things done	135
17	Spotting an opportunity and standing out	141
18	Sucking it up	149
19	Pushing back and saying 'no'	157
20	Working out when to leave	167

Part V: The leadership track		**175**
21	Setting priorities	179
22	The importance of delegating	187
23	Building your leadership confidence	195
24	The work–life balance myth	203
25	Leadership—it's personal	209

| *Conclusion* | *215* |
| *Index* | *217* |

ABOUT ALEX MALLEY

Source: © CPA Australia

Alex Malley FCPA is the CEO of CPA Australia and is responsible for 19 offices globally with more than 150 000 members in 121 countries.

Alex was born in Sydney, Australia, to immigrant parents. From the time he and his family remember, he was a disruptive boy—ever curious about all around him.

His life and career have been extremely diverse, with experiences that include banking, sports management, university lecturing, media commentary as well as roles as CEO, board director and chairmanship roles.

Tackling leadership and mentoring matters is something he has always taken very seriously. As host of the television series *The Bottom Line*, screened nationally on the Nine Network Australia, Alex brings these issues into sharp focus through interviews with fellow leaders from business, politics and the community. The interview he conducted with the first man on the moon, Neil Armstrong, was the most substantive ever filmed. News surrounding it reached an unprecedented global audience.

Alex fronts the online mentoring community for students, thenakedceo.com. Approximately two million young people have visited the site to date. The extraordinary engagement achieved on the website was the inspiration behind this book— *The Naked CEO: The truth you need to build a big life.*

He writes a regular blog for *The Huffington Post* and is a business commentator on the nationally syndicated programs *Money News* on 2GB and *Sky News Business.*

Alex serves on a number of councils, boards and government sector committees including the Prince of Wales' Accounting for Sustainability Project and the International Integrated Reporting Council domiciled in London.

In recent times, Alex was invited to become a LinkedIn Influencer: part of an exclusive group of global leaders, which includes the likes of Richard Branson, Bill Gates and US President Barack Obama. Via regular blog posts, Alex shares his leadership insights with LinkedIn's network of more than 300 million professionals around the globe.

From suspended schoolboy to disruptive CEO, Alex has always done what he believes in.

ACKNOWLEDGEMENTS

I wish to acknowledge the Board of CPA Australia for their vision to encourage creative freedom in the quest to guide future generations. We are also blessed with an outstanding CPA Australia staff who continue to overachieve in all they do—thank you colleagues for your dedication and belief.

Thank you Jillian Bowen for your passion, drive and work ethic for this mission and to The Naked CEO website and university teams in particular. And to Kristen Hammond at Wiley for your initiative and encouragement of this book.

In a world that is in desperate need of more generous leaders, I wish to acknowledge the extraordinary group of people who shared their words of support at the beginning of this book, which is a true reflection of their desire to also encourage future generations.

SPECIAL THANKS

To Jonathan Abbott for helping me bring this book to life—I will not quickly forget the many hours at the dining room table surrounded by notes, laptops, coffees and fruit. Thank you for bringing your talent, good grace and good fun with you.

PROLOGUE

This book shares the career and leadership principles that I worked out the hard way on my journey from suspended schoolboy to CEO. It's also my challenge to you to go out into the world and test what you are capable of. Dare to throw yourself into experiences. It does not matter if you stumble or fall; we all do. But promise me you will never live your life in fear of failure. I want you to have a big life.

Let's start from my humble beginnings. In my final year of school I was suspended—here is how it happened.

I went to an all-boys school. One day, a friend of mine claimed he had a girlfriend. You have to understand that in the seventies, at an all-boys school, such a claim was pretty big news, and I couldn't just take my friend's word for it—I needed evidence.

Never shy of an adventure and always keen to disrupt the daily routine, I was only too happy to offer to drive him to the city so we could meet her. So, soon after the lunchtime bell blared, my partner in crime and I, along with a couple of others, were in my bright-orange Datsun confident we'd made a clean getaway.

As it turned out, the girlfriend did exist.

After a few hours of nothing much, for me at least, we decided it was time to get back. So no teachers would see us, we parked at the back of the school, scaled the fence and darted across the rugby fields towards class. The classroom fell silent when we entered. All eyes were fixed on us. Then, with a deadpan delivery, the teacher informed us not to bother finding a seat because the headmaster wanted to see us immediately.

Alarmed, we reluctantly followed orders.

Waiting to be called into the headmaster's office was an excruciating torment. Mr West (the headmaster) let us stew outside for what seemed like at least an hour before eventually calling us in. He then wasted no time in bluntly informing us that we had been spotted sprinting to my car and zooming out of the car park—a teacher had witnessed the entire great escape from his classroom window. I meekly contested that it had not been us, but with my afro hairstyle and orange car I may as well have been wearing a shirt with 'Alex Malley' printed on the back.

Quickly we came to terms with the fact that there was no escape. We had been caught. Mr West handed us our letters of suspension and gestured towards the door with a stiff nod. We left the office, devastated.

Immediately my mum came to my mind. She suffered from chronic depression and this sort of stress was something she could definitely do without. But I knew I had to tell her—so I did. She was okay about it, but we did not think my dad would be. So we decided not to tell him. Every day of my suspension I arrived at the breakfast table dressed in my school uniform, left at the usual time and returned to the dinner table with pre-prepared tales of what I had learnt at school that day. I didn't tell Dad about the suspension until I was 21 when the dust was long settled. Even then he was unimpressed, and fair enough—he deserved better from me.

While this situation was awful at the time, many years on I recount that moment in my life with a level of appreciation. My decision that day, albeit misguided and, ultimately, a big mistake, taught me multiple lessons.

We all make mistakes and it is what we learn from them that matters most. With time on my hands it dawned on me that, living with Mum's depression, school and my friends were actually a secure place for me. In those days of real isolation, I reflected on the fact that I was wasting a real opportunity. As strange as it may seem, during that time I decided I wanted to become a teacher. I wanted to make the classroom interesting, somewhere students wanted to be. I wrote a note to myself about this and kept it—then and there, I made a commitment to myself.

Many years later, after a number of mistakes and misadventures (some of which I share with you in this book), I walked on stage to receive from the then Minister for Education, Science and Training, Brendan Nelson, a national university teaching honour. On the front of my citation was the note I wrote to myself while on suspension.

Some goals take time to achieve. Always remember, you will ultimately reach them if they mean enough to you.

I stayed in touch with Mr West and today he is a friend. He is also never short on advice—even if I don't ask for it! This shows that in life we never know how things will end up. A momentary combatant became, for me, a lifelong friend. With an open mind, remember—anything can happen.

Sadly, I no longer sport the afro. I imagine my Datsun has long since become scrap metal, but the spirit of stretching the rules, experiencing new things and disrupting routines has never left me. Sure, I am more mature and I have learnt a lot since then but, deep down, I am still that boy.

Staying true to who you are is no easy feat. Working out who you are is even harder. Life is about growth—exposing yourself to different experiences helps you learn more about the world but, more relevantly, about yourself.

Many people feel it necessary to become someone else. I think that is incredibly sad. Much of the essence of who you are, in my view, comes from your earliest years. You should never let the good things go, no matter the environment or circumstance you enter into. Thankfully I know this now, but I think myself lucky to have worked this out, because no-one ever told me this was the case. If someone were to ask me what my biggest regrets are, I would say I don't have many, except for never having had someone to mentor me early in my life and career. Over many years, I worked with a lot of great leaders but they kept their wisdom and insight close to their chests.

So here I am today, a leader, determined to share my mistakes and earned insights. Through my experiences, the good and the bad,

I have learnt a few things about professional life and leadership that I want to share with you, one of the next generation, in the hope you might draw something beneficial from them.

Rather than take a small-scale route, I decided to create this book as my investment into the spirit of youth, and offer a complete, no-holds-barred perspective on career progression and leadership. It is not a book of answers. Answers can only come from your own experiences in life. It is not a sugar-coated version of life in the workplace. I would be doing you a major disservice if it was. It is not full of prescribed leadership techniques, because everyone's journey is different and leadership is personal.

This is a guide. The more open-minded you are, the richer you will find this book.

While you're reading, I encourage you to go back to your earliest memories of what gave you a buzz, what made you excited, what made you feel at home. What was it? Was it the sound of sport? Was it acting in the school play? Was it a book or movie? I ask this of you because our earliest instincts, what made us happy, are a big part of who we are. So as you consider the life ahead of you, promise me you will first go back and answer those questions so you can build on this foundation. Bring yourself back to your instincts—it will help you move forward. Our passions drive us. Let them help to navigate you on your work and life journey. It may take time, but persist.

For me, writing a book is as hard as it gets. Confining myself to one spot for a set period of time is something I have always struggled with. Doing so is pretty much the antithesis of who I am and what I do. But I believe in a leader's responsibility to impart their experience and insight. I put my personal unease aside in the hope that this book guides you along your adventure.

This book traverses the transition from the educational environment to the workplace, right through to being a leader and all that entails. No matter your experience in the workplace or stage of leadership today, you will find something valuable in this book. It is written to stay relevant for you into the future and will provide different insights to you over time as your experiences develop. Whether you're a school or university student or a young professional, your career is in transition or you're a parent, something personal is in this book for you.

It is structured into five sections which cover the themes that my experiences indicate will best place you on your leadership journey—from dreaming to finding the leadership role of your dreams.

This book is an extension of The Naked CEO website you may have already visited. To date, over two million people have. If you have any questions about your career after reading this book, you can reach me via the Ask Alex section at thenakedceo.com and **I will personally respond to your question via video**, as I have done for the past three years on the site.

That is my personal commitment to you.

So what are your dreams?

PART I
DARE TO DREAM

When I was twenty-two years old, I marched out of a job interview convinced I had destroyed my career.

I was in the running for what I believed was my dream job. After a lot of preparation and a series of gruelling interviews, I was elated when the interviewer called to inform me that I was one of only two applicants left in contention. I knew from conversations that well over one hundred people had applied for the position, so the fact I had made it to this stage instilled me with a lot of confidence.

Unfortunately, my confidence was fleeting.

At my prospective employer's offices, the interviewer informed me that as part of the final selection process, I would need to complete what's known today as a psychometric test. Without really knowing why, my palms turned sweaty and my heart began to race. I felt afraid for the first time in the whole interview process. When the examiner placed the test papers on the desk in front of me and triggered her stopwatch, I picked up a pen with a trembling hand. But I couldn't process a clear thought, let alone write. Panic had overcome me. Soon I shot up, declared I couldn't do it and rushed out of the room.

Head low, dazed and miserable, I walked out onto the street, convinced I'd find no way back from this embarrassment. An instant of inexplicable fear had wrecked my otherwise excellent chances of securing my dream job, and it had surely destroyed any possibility of me achieving any other. People talk: I would be known as that person who had cracked under pressure. The person who did not have what it took to be a professional.

Sandwiched between people on the train ride home, I looked around. Everyone was in their own world, completely oblivious of me. I was anonymous. And if I'm anonymous, I thought, surely I am free to make mistakes. Really, my only critic was myself—other people were focused on their own lives, not mine. The examiner was probably back at her desk focused on something else and I would soon be forgotten. So the only person making a big deal out of my botched performance was me. If I could overcome it, turn it into something positive, something I could learn from, there was no reason I couldn't put this whole ordeal behind me, and move on and up.

So that is what I did. I stepped off the train with my head held high, and I kept it high even when the inevitable phone call came to inform me that I had not got the job.

After years of reflection, I now know where my fear stemmed from that day. When I was twelve years old, my teacher asked me to complete a similar sort of test. My friends and I didn't know what this surprise test was, so didn't take it seriously. We laughed and whispered the entire way through it. Subsequently, my teacher called my parents to inform them that I would be dropped to a lower level class due to my poor result. Naturally I felt embarrassed and deflated, and, although I hadn't known it at the time, it was the memory of those feelings that took control of me on the day I ran away from the test. This just goes to show how previous negative experiences in life can potentially impact your future. But they don't need to—you can change their impact with the right attitude. Start working on that today.

What began as a disaster on that day quickly became the best thing that ever happened to me in my career. It was a turning point that set me on a course I have never deviated from: one where I never let fear and embarrassment get in the way of my dreams. They are useless emotions. They will hold you back from achieving your aspirations. If you can delete them from your mind from a young age, you will start the real journey of life a lot sooner than those people who let such emotions drive them.

No hurdle is insurmountable. Never let fear of a challenge stop you. At times during your career, you may feel under pressure to change who you are as a person to meet someone else's expectation. Don't. Too many people lose their daring nature, let go of their childlike mind, and curb their behaviour and dreams because they feel they have to when they 'grow up'. They become consumed with a fear of failure, so they simply toe the proverbial line. That is the worst thing you can do.

Even now, I possess the same childish, imaginative, silly mind that I had when I was seventeen, and this has played a huge part in my career ascendency. Yes, you should be respectful. Polite. Personal. Disciplined. Learn to be an effective communicator. But never feel growing up means you have to compromise who you are or what you really want in life.

Make dreaming a habit. And never let go of your daring and drive to actualise those dreams.

CHAPTER 1

BE YOURSELF

'Just be yourself.' I'm sure you've heard this before, but have you really thought about it from a career perspective?

The ability to be true to oneself is the most underrated and overlooked mindset for people at the start of their career and throughout their life. Too many people fall into the trap of projecting a distorted image of themselves, because they feel doing so is necessary to meet someone else's expectation, someone else's ideal. Young professionals often get so entrenched in changing their personality or behaviour to meet the perceived expectation of a boss or colleagues that they lose what makes them special: themselves.

There is one truth: being authentic is the master key to a positive life and career. Facades are a risky and exhausting business.

Having worked with many people in my lifetime, a huge turnoff for me has always been the person sitting across the desk with their guard up so high they are like some sort of pre-programmed robot. I understand that the early years in business can be nerve-wracking, but you should know that what your manager and colleagues are looking for is really quite simple: that you will be good to work and live with, possess a willingness to take instruction, and have an eagerness to learn. Those attributes can only be accurately determined when you exhibit your true self.

We all have a finite amount of mental and physical energy. So in work and life, it is important to concentrate your energy on the things that matter, the things that will earn you respect as an effective employee and colleague. Do not waste your energy trying to mould your personality into something you're not, or modelling it on someone else. You will only exhaust yourself and, subsequently, your effectiveness will begin to suffer.

In your life you will go through many interviews and professional situations where people will be judging you. I can confidently tell you that, in the vast majority of cases, the core of your success (or otherwise) will depend on whether they feel they know you as a person, that you are authentic.

Sure, chances are not everyone will respond to you, but you will earn a level of respect and trust, which are essential to progressing your career and achieving you dreams.

You should think of yourself as a brand—brand 'You'. That brand will grow as you grow. No-one is like you. Accentuate that and sell that. Don't try to be like anyone else. Always ask yourself: what are my positive characteristics? What can I enhance? What are the challenges I need to overcome? What is it I need to do to improve?

Let yourself shine—it is a key part of what life is about and what those around you will come to respect and enjoy.

MAKE IT HAPPEN: HOW TO BE YOURSELF

Authentic people are always respected, but not always liked. If you can only have one of those two characteristics said of you, take being respected every time. People too often confuse popularity with success and this is a big mistake.

To be yourself, know yourself

Throughout your life you will face good, bad and ugly circumstances, but your reaction to those circumstances will tell you more about who you are—your character, your strengths and the things you need to be better at. The more you experience life, the more you learn about yourself. So, for now, expose yourself to as many life experiences as you can.

Why not write down what you consider to be your three best personal attributes, along with the three things you need to be better at? Plant those traits in your mind, and recognise and practise them in every aspect of your life. Identify how your friends, family members and colleagues respond when you are exhibiting either one of your positive or one of your negative attributes. This will help you understand how people perceive you, and why they react to you in a certain manner in a particular moment. This is the beginning of developing your self-awareness. Understanding how your behaviour impacts others is incredibly important in truly getting to the core of who you are. Self-awareness is one of the most important qualities an effective leader should possess.

Stop keeping up with the Joneses

For many, the temptation to compare oneself with others is difficult to overcome. While it is okay to admire others' achievements, the only person's development you should be concerned with is your own. Do not compare yourself to others, but seek to be the best that you can be. Focus on how your strengths, your unique DNA, can help you achieve your goals. Always be gracious about success and be willing to share your learnings with others.

Do unto others

You learn a lot about a person by the way they treat others. Understand, however, that if someone reacts poorly or is dismissive of your ideas, they could be dealing with issues that you're unaware of, hence that reaction.

Do your best to remain positive with all people, be kind whenever you can, remember and use people's names, show an honest interest in their welfare, and always be constructive even in circumstances where you may have to be critical.

Honesty is the best policy

Be honest and open with the people around you. Remember, honesty starts with you. Look within yourself at your own flaws and mistakes and own them. It is refreshing to meet people who accept responsibility and are accountable for their actions. Honest and open people are the ones most likely to be trusted with senior responsibilities.

Just let it go

In the ebbs and flows of life, avoid being too self-critical about your performance. In your memory of many of those circumstances, you will have exaggerated the issues because you are too close to them. It is always important to step away, let go of the negative emotions, and put the issues in real context. Forgive yourself. Think about how you can be better. You can learn much from your past, but the most important lesson is not to keep living there.

Stop worrying about whether people like you

No matter how hard you try, not everyone is going to like you, so stop worrying about what other people think of you. Be self-aware and evaluate other people's feedback and critiques, but break the cycle of letting negativity undermine the development of your talents. When you receive negative feedback, use it to make yourself a stronger and better person.

Find some stress relief

Take a deep breath. It is common to worry about what will happen in important and high-pressure situations. But think about the last time you were really worried about something. Was the most unpleasant part of the experience the worrying, rather than the actual outcome? In almost every circumstance of life, when we reflect on previous experiences that we thought were intolerable, we often laugh at how seriously we took the issue and ourselves at the time.

Put your unique DNA on display—be brand 'You'

Have you ever stopped to consider just how incredibly unique we all are in a world of billions of people? And yet, so many of us spend our lives mimicking others—whether that means buying similar clothes, or having similar hobbies or lifestyles.

Instead, focus on brand 'You': the universe has only one such product. Show me your personality, your quirks, your humour. Show me what makes you interesting and unique. If you want to be heard and recognised, promote brand 'You'.

Quotable quote from Alex

Young professionals often get so entrenched in changing their personality or behaviour to meet the perceived expectation of a boss or colleagues that they lose what makes them special: themselves.

There is one truth: being authentic is the master key to a positive life and career. Facades are a risky and exhausting business.

Stop trying to please everyone

Apart from being really exhausting, trying to please everyone can be a truly thankless task. Making others happy is nice, but not to the point where you are always last in line. Helping others and trying to please them should be something that happens naturally. If it's something you're overly focused on or, worse still, worrying about, you're trying too hard.

Follow your instinct

Have you ever done something and afterwards chastised yourself because you knew it was the wrong thing to do? That is your intuition or instinct talking. And in many cases, only you and your instinct truly know the answer to an important question in your life. So stop and listen. If you don't like the answer, sleep on it. If your instinct gives you the same answer every time you ask the question, it's probably onto something.

DON'T FORGET

Here are the main points to remember from this chapter:

- learn from the past and look to the future
- invest your energies into the things that matter—pretending to be someone you're not isn't one of those
- stop worrying about what other people think
- put your unique self on display when going for jobs—show brand 'You'.

Get ahead of the pack

Want to get more out of this process? Here are some ideas:

- *Do it:* Keep a basic journal and record the things you were successful with and the things you want to focus on improving. Review your journal regularly as a reminder of who you are becoming and the progress you have made.

- *Ask yourself:* Are you creative? Emotional? Logical? Organised? Think about which areas are your strengths and which are your weaknesses, and discuss them with trusted colleagues as you learn to work together as a stronger team.

Meet the mentee: Chad Walker

As father of two Chad Walker approached graduation from James Cook University, he wondered if being a little older than most in his cohort would make it difficult to compete with other Bachelor of Business graduates.

He met with Alex to discuss his career and to seek some advice.

The most important takeaway he received from the session was an understanding that his biggest asset was being comfortable about being himself. Alex encouraged him to hold on to it and exhibit it consistently.

Chad noted: 'Instead of seeing my scattered history as a negative representation of myself, Alex told me to remember that the breadth of experience I've had means that I'm an entirely different kind of accountant than anyone else, with a different experience. I'm not just interested in numbers, and it gives me a bit of perspective on things.

'I can become a person of influence by being myself and sharing my experiences, without necessarily making my way to the top of a company. I know I've made mistakes. I know where I've come from. I know what I think is right and what's not right. Alex reminded me that I don't have to hide those experiences and opinions; I can be true to myself, and have the integrity to stand up for what I believe in and support people from any role.'

This attitude helped Chad to recently make some significant career decisions. When the head of his work team unexpectedly resigned, Chad was presented with the opportunity to move up into the role on a temporary basis. Chad admits it was a big step up.

'In my old way of thinking, I would have simply thought that I was unqualified for an accounting role at that level. But Alex's words helped me to see my skillset more holistically. I have the accounting knowledge from my studies. And even though I don't have management experience in the accounting profession, I've managed teams in a retail setting; I've got people skills, and I've got life skills.'

Although the role is only temporary, Chad acknowledges that taking on the job was a huge career leap and doing so has helped him to learn a lot about himself, his strengths, and where he would like to be in the future. The experience has served as evidence that being yourself can really pay off.

The mentoring session with Alex also helped Chad to realise that his goal was not to be elected to a position of power or leadership, but to be the type of person who can make a difference and influence others no matter what their title is.

CHAPTER 2

DREAMS DON'T HAPPEN OVERNIGHT

Dreams are not just nice thoughts and fantasies. They are a mindset, a habit, a call to action and something to strive towards. Achieving them requires vision, passion and a lot of hard work. The dreams you really want to achieve are the ones you think about all the time. The ones you remember.

Never be afraid to build your dreams—accept the fact that if you are going to lead a big, exciting life, you will make mistakes, but these will likely teach you something about yourself that you did not know before. Don't ever let a fear of mistakes or failure hold you back from your dreams.

Understand that the journey to your dreams will likely take you into an unfamiliar stratosphere, away from your comfort zone, and perhaps even force you to undertake actions that are unnatural to you. That's okay—it is all part of the ride. If you understand this is going on, stepping into the unknown will become more exciting than it is intimidating.

If the dream is something you really want, let it linger in your mind—that way, you will never miss identifying the opportunity to convert it into reality. This opportunity will come—guaranteed. But will you recognise it? It may not appear dressed exactly as you think.

Working towards your dreams will test your resolve. It will challenge your patience. But it is important to understand and remember that most big dreams take time to actualise. I am middle-aged, and while I have worked hard to achieve some of my dreams, I can sincerely tell you that I am unconcerned that I am yet to achieve them all.

Knowing the opportunity to do so could be as soon as tomorrow keeps me hungry.

Reality check: there might be a time where you reach a dream, only to realise it is actually not something you want. Perhaps it's not everything you had hoped it would be. This has happened to me. I have always loved sport, so as a young man I pursued and attained my dream of working in sports management. After some time, I began to realise that, as much as I loved sport, I did not want it to be my career—I wanted to keep it as a personal passion. Over the course of the experience I met many great people, and had invested and learnt a lot, so I felt comfortable when I decided to move on to my next career adventure.

Once you have reached a dream, it's okay to pull out of it—just make sure you're not doing it for the wrong reasons, and definitely don't let it become a habit. Consistently hitting the eject button on your way to, or once you have reached, a dream may cause you and others to doubt your ability, commitment and resolve. So, if you pull out of a dream, do so only when you know you have given it your best shot.

Not sure what your dreams are yet? Well, to that I say: you are not trying hard enough. Open your mind to the world around you; listen; ask yourself what you're looking for, what makes you happy. And in there somewhere you will find that dream or vision. Now all that is left is to set a course towards achieving it.

MAKE IT HAPPEN: HOW TO ACHIEVE YOUR DREAMS

We know that most dreams don't happen overnight. So, to give yourself the best chance of achieving those really big dreams that you should be thinking about, it is important to learn how to set goals. Goals are the building blocks in developing the required discipline to reach those big dreams.

But how can you define exactly what your goals are and motivate yourself to work towards them? The following provides some tips that have worked for me.

Capture your goals

To help get your goal off the ground, write it down on a piece of paper and stick it on the wall above your desk. Add pictures of what the ambition looks like to you. The more you surround yourself with your goal, the more you will be reminded to stay on track.

Make sure your goals are achievable

Working towards a goal that is unlikely to be reached, at least at this point in time, is wasted energy. It may even unnecessarily dent your confidence. If your objective is currently unachievable, be honest and accept that. You can still keep it on your list of possibilities, but think about working on the more immediate and attainable steps leading towards the ultimate goal.

Picture success

Use your imagination to visualise the moment when you have reached your ambition. This will not only keep you motivated and focused, but may also help you think about new ways of achieving success.

Get advice and support

Do you know someone who has the experience or qualifications to assist you? Start talking to them, and seek out their advice and support. If you're having trouble finding such a person, do some investigating and don't be afraid to reach out to someone you may have only read about or seen on television. You will never know if they're willing to impart their insights if you don't ask.

Be realistic

Setting a realistic time frame is important. Declaring what you will achieve 'one day' is pointless if you don't know when 'one day' is. Choose a time frame and do your best to stick to it. If you reach the end of that time line and the goal is yet to be achieved, it's decision-making time. Do you extend your time frame, or is your goal unattainable?

Break your goal down

Sometimes a goal seems too big to achieve, but when you break it down into a sequence of smaller targets the possibilities may become clearer. Think of each target as a building block towards your final destination.

Persevere

You may have heard the phrase popularised by William Edward Hickson: 'If at first you don't succeed, try, try, try again.' Working towards a goal is often challenging, because you may well need to pursue a few different avenues to achieve it. As obstacles arise, you must always work on maintaining your self-belief that there is a solution.

Quotable quote from Alex

Working towards your dreams will test your resolve. It will challenge your patience. But it is important to understand and remember that most big dreams take time to actualise.

Know when to be flexible

Try to maintain a flexible mindset. Flexibility can take the form of seeking different advice, adding additional steps or refining the goal. But ensure you don't use flexibility as an excuse for procrastination.

Celebrate success

You have set your mind to achieving something and now you have. Celebrate. Rewarding yourself, especially if it has been an arduous journey to get to this point, will create a positive mental association that will likely increase your motivation to achieve future goals.

DON'T FORGET

Remember these important insights from this chapter:

- don't be afraid to dream big
- set a realistic time line to reach your goals
- remember things don't always go to plan—be patient and persist
- always be on the lookout for opportunities to actualise your goals.

Get ahead of the pack

Here's how to really follow your dreams:

- *Do it:* Give yourself the best chance to form a dream. Start reading newspapers, magazine and websites looking for topics that interest you. If you persist you will find something that you choose to pursue. Tell someone what your dream is as soon as you choose and define it, and ask them to regularly check with you what you're doing to achieve it.

- *Ask yourself:* Is the dream you've always had still firmly in your mind in spite of time elapsing? If it is, that's likely a good sign—it's persisting. So what are you doing about it?

Meet the mentee: Anand Jakate

Anand Jakate was working as a registered nurse in Canberra. For some time he had been considering a career change so he conducted some research and came across The Naked CEO website. He read and watched Alex's conversations about the power of dreams and Alex's statements that he himself had pursued many.

Anand reached out to Alex via Facebook and asked: 'I'm a registered nurse working in an Australian hospital but I have developed an interest in becoming an accountant, so I am thinking of enrolling to complete my Master of Professional Accounting. I am already 26. Does this sound crazy or risky? Is it too late to start?'

Alex provided him with some very straightforward guidance with the overall theme being to 'chase your passions'.

After taking this advice on board, Anand enrolled in the Masters of Professional Accounting at the University of Canberra and pursued volunteer work experience in accounting roles in India where his parents live.

Now eighteen months after first contacting Alex, Anand has completed his master's program and first exam in the CPA Program and is positioned to embark on a new chapter in his career journey. He hopes to obtain a graduate role at a Big 4 firm, like PwC or Deloitte, and his overarching dream is to attain a management position in the auditing or advisory sector of the accounting profession.

Although Anand had planned to start a long-term career a little earlier in his life, he is happy that he went back to university to change career paths. Anand's story is a great example of maintaining your dreams and recognising that they will not happen overnight.

CHAPTER 3

MISTAKES MAKE YOU SMARTER AND STRONGER

When a decision you have made, or a course you have taken, turns out to be the wrong one, you have not made a mistake, you have made a friend. Why do I believe this? Well, friends can make you stronger and friends can make you smarter. And that is exactly what mistakes do, too.

When you're faced with an undesirable outcome that you're responsible for, make it known that you have accepted the responsibility. Don't shy away from it or pretend you were not to blame. Acknowledging it will immediately make you stronger.

This takes courage, and obviously you want to make as few mistakes as possible, but at the same time they will teach you a lot about the significance of accountability: an essential quality for any employee and future leader. Walking into an office to tell your boss or colleagues that you have made a mistake, while daunting, builds enormous character. It strengthens the foundation you are building your career on.

Mistakes also make you smarter. You will learn from them, and you will find out how to accept and move on from them. Eating 'humble pie' once in a while does not always have to taste bad. What is important is that you are extending yourself enough to even take the chance of making a mistake.

With the expectation of learning, you have to possess a willingness to try things and, as a result of trying, you will make mistakes. Everyone who desires to reach their dreams and live a full life will make mistakes along the way.

But then there are those people who consistently drive through life with the windows up, the doors closed and locked, because they are afraid of taking chances. They have learnt nothing about their capability. They have not grown as people. They have stayed so safe that they have made no productive effort to have a big life full of unique, character-building experiences. To me, that is not life.

Every time you make a mistake, you will discover how resilient you are. You will learn more about your character and how well, or how badly, you cope when you don't perform at your expectation. Talking to your boss or colleagues about complex and unpleasant issues are daily undertakings for a leader, so facing your mistakes and learning how to communicate to others is essential for your professional development.

More often than not, those people brave enough to take calculated risks to achieve bigger things are far more impressive and stronger as people.

When someone tells me they have never made a mistake, what they are really telling me is they have never lived.

MAKE IT HAPPEN: HOW TO LEARN FROM YOUR MISTAKES

Here are some tips to help you accept and learn from your mistakes, and grow stronger—and then move on.

Be honest and own it

You have made a mistake—now what? The best way to start turning it into a positive is to admit you have made it. When you start blaming other people, you distance yourself from any possible lesson. So if you did the wrong thing, accept that while it is not going to be pleasant, you will recover. And it is unlikely you will make that same mistake again.

Reflect on what went wrong

Take a few minutes to work out what happened. Once you have got your head around it, think about what you could do differently if you found yourself in the same situation in the future. If you're struggling to understand the situation, ask a mentor or someone you trust with more experience for their input.

Look at the glass as half full

You'll achieve little from thinking about mistakes as failures rather than opportunities to learn and grow as a person. In fact, people are often more likely to learn from their mistakes than their successes. With each mistake you make, you're able to learn a lot more about yourself, other people and practical processes that will help you in the future.

Know how to avoid unnecessary mistakes

If you make a mistake because you didn't understand what was required of you at the outset, I would classify this as an avoidable or unnecessary mistake. Always ask questions so you understand the task or directive before embarking on it. You may feel you're losing face by saying, 'I don't understand', but this will be fleeting compared to what the alternative could end up being.

Find solutions

I find it disappointing when someone who has contributed to a mistake does not consider how to fix it before raising it with me. The negativity surrounding the issue may be minimised when the problem and possible solution are offered at the same time.

Taking a moment to solve the problem, or at least making an effort to do so, will garner you a lot more respect from your managers and colleagues. Think through the issue rationally and objectively. Ask yourself: What caused the mistake? Who will need to be made aware of it? And what is a potential solution?

Stay calm

Letting stress and fear take control can be easy when something goes wrong, but being guided by these emotions will probably just dig you a deeper hole. So when you make a mistake, remain calm and composed, and avoid making impulsive decisions to remedy the situation.

Quotable quote from Alex

Walking into an office to tell your boss or colleagues that you have made a mistake, while daunting, builds enormous character. It strengthens the foundation you are building your career on.

Keep things in perspective

Think about some of the mistakes you have made in your life already. Consider what you learnt from the experience and how your emotions shifted over time. I smile when remembering the mistakes I made as a young professional, chiefly because at the time they seemed so completely catastrophic. Now they are vestiges of my early career—I look back on them with appreciation and, often times, amusement.

Accept other's behaviours

Being judgemental is one of the worst traits of humanity. When someone else makes a mistake, which may or may not affect you, remember that these things can happen to anyone, and it will likely be your turn one day. Try to look upon these circumstances as an opportunity for you to exhibit your generosity of spirit by helping the colleague fix and move on from their error. This approach could completely redefine your relationship with that colleague, turning it into something much more positive.

Move on when the time is right

Once you have acknowledged and accepted the consequences, it is time to move on. The world lives in the moment and aims for the future. In that context, it is important your confidence and judgement remain positive. Do not be tentative about future decisions based on what may have happened in the past. The great achievers in life have enormous bounce-back capacity.

Take some time for later reflections

As a CEO, I value an open and creative workplace. The people I work with know that in the process of trying to achieve great things, some things may go wrong. This culture is encouraged because I remember what it was like working in an environment that was unforgiving about anything other than perfection, and because I know perfection is unattainable.

When you take on leadership roles, never forget the value of insight that is gained from your missteps and be prepared to let others make them.

DON'T FORGET

Here are the main steps to take after making a mistake:

- be accountable
- work out what went wrong and learn from it
- provide a recommended solution to the mistake
- don't let the mistake damage your self-confidence.

Get ahead of the pack

Here are some tips to ramp up your learning and get ahead of the pack:

- *Add it up:* According to a 2011 study by the *International Journal of Research in Management and Technology*, between 70 and 90 per cent of all mistakes in the workplace are the result of human error. So, as much as it is tempting to blame technology, most of the time it actually is our mistake.

- *Ask yourself:* Have you ever made a mistake and said, 'I'm sorry you feel that way'? That is not an apology. If you truly made the mistake, be accountable for the action.

Meet the mentee: Demara Roche

UTS accounting student Demara Roche met Alex when she featured in an episode of The Naked CEO. During a one-on-one mentoring session she shared her fear of failure and lack of confidence when it came to making big decisions.

During the mentoring, Alex told Demara that 'no-one makes all the right decisions in life; it's normal to make some mistakes. Aim to be the best at what you love doing and everything else will fall into place.'

After receiving Alex's advice, Demara started applying for jobs that she says she was not quite qualified for — not just to gain employment, but for the experience of putting together job applications that she was proud of and practising interview techniques. She says the process helped her to figure out how to present herself in a more confident way.

'In my session with Alex I was told "If you're not making mistakes, you're not trying hard enough because it means you're not pushing boundaries." Hearing that so plainly really shocked me into not being too scared to try things I thought were out of reach,' said Demara.

Demara also sought out different volunteer opportunities and ways to gain additional experience within the accounting profession. She took on a role as a CPA Australia student ambassador at university, and also signed up for a leadership role within her university's student business society.

Since spending time with Alex, Demara has faced some tough decisions in her personal life. She said that without Alex's advice and guidance she wasn't sure that she would have been able to face those challenges.

'I think a lot of my new-found confidence has to do with knowing that Alex has encouraged me to take risks and opportunities and just to try things and to know that really nothing is going to go wrong,' said Demara.

CHAPTER 4

INSIGHTS COME FROM EVERYWHERE

As a child, playing with my friends meant a lot more to me than just having fun: it was an escape. This was because my mother suffered from clinical depression. Knowing she was not well was a very hard reality to grow up in.

On one particular day when I was about 13 years old, I was at my mother's bedside in the hospital waiting for her to wake up. Various doctors and nurses came in to check on her, but they didn't talk to me. No-one who appeared to have any sort of rank or seniority said a thing. I guess I had spent so much time there I had become a little like a part of the furniture. But then a cleaner came in to mop the floor. After a short time he caught my eye and smiled as he said something to the effect of, 'You must be Alex. Your mother has told me all about how much she loves you and your brother and sisters. I think your mother is great—you are lucky to have her.' And that was it: he went on his way. But that's all he needed to say.

I have reflected on that memory many times over the course of my life. It was so brief, but so poignant. That gentleman gave me a sense of my mother and myself. He made me feel comfortable about the difficult circumstance I was in by speaking to me with respect and kindness. And he gave me a renewed appreciation that insight can come from anyone, at any time.

Insight does not always come from someone in a senior position, someone with more experience, someone you would expect. Keep an open ear and mind when it comes to the people you listen to. The more you listen to all of those around you, the better you will become at filtering through the noise to find those nuggets of gold that you can learn from. It comes down to developing a feeling for the environment around you—this is one of the skills you have to develop in your life.

I have learnt to respect all people. It has been a key part of my life and management approach for many years. Respecting people allows you to live within a more positive world where additional insights are gleaned by the other person's comfort in you, because they know you respect them.

Every person in the world has a perspective worth listening to. Insights really do come from everywhere.

Insights from others will provide the stimulus to further develop your own knowledge, ideas, creativity and emotion. The challenge is to create the relationships and circumstances to attract such insights. All around you the opportunity to learn abounds—but are you looking?

MAKE IT HAPPEN: HOW TO FIND INSIGHTS

Here's how to find the insights and resources that inspire you.

Know that resources abound

You really can find insights anywhere. Read articles or stories about people and their achievements that you find inspiring. Attend events, watch a documentary or see a movie that excites you and gets your creativity flowing. Think about what made what you have seen or heard so special.

Here is my favourite thing to do: have a different conversation with your parents or friends about their life experiences, and what made them do the things they did in their life.

Speak to the heart—welcome to a whole new world.

Be inventive

Why do some people have great idea after great idea, like it just comes naturally to them? I can tell you, while many of those people are naturally creative, they also possess an ability to absorb like a sponge. This process makes them confident and opportunistic.

A good starting exercise is to take a successful idea you have read or heard about, and then give yourself the creative freedom to write down what you would do to make it even more impactful. This will help create a healthy habit of expanding your mind.

Capture your ideas

Do you get frustrated because the new ideas that come to you do so at inconvenient times, like in the middle of the night, or when you're at the supermarket or catching public transport? To avoid forgetting them, carry a pad and pen, or have a notes app on your phone, so you can record your ideas any time they arrive.

Value every environment

I often start a conversation with people I don't know, and I do so in various environments. It might be with the person I'm sitting next to on a plane or at a sporting event, for instance. Sometimes listening to the perspectives or story of someone from outside your day-to-day life can spark fresh inspiration.

While at work, if you're struggling to be creative, change your environment. Find a dedicated space where you are undistracted, or go for a walk to clear your mind and think freely.

Break down barriers

Try a ten-minute free-writing session about a topic that interests you. Free-writing is where you write down anything that comes into your mind about a particular topic during a set time. Don't read or change anything during the free-writing session—just keep writing until the time is up.

> ### Quotable quote from Alex
>
> Insight does not always come from someone in a senior position, someone with more experience, someone you would expect. Keep an open ear and mind when it comes to the people you listen to... Every person in the world has a perspective worth listening to. Insights really do come from everywhere.

Hone your observation skills

On many occasions after an important meeting I have asked my colleagues to recount to me what they observed in body language and communication. The reason I do this is because people often speak more clearly through their body movement than they do through their words. Sometimes you have to work hard to observe feelings and obtain insights, rather than hear them.

So start asking yourself why things are the way they are around you. The key to this exercise is asking questions. The more curious you are, the more insights you will absorb, and hopefully the more ideas you will generate.

Not everyone wants to play

I have discovered over time that not everyone is willing to share their personal insights or ideas. Not surprisingly, they may also be uninterested in yours. Learn to recognise that in other people—although I have always tried to make it a personal challenge to influence them to change, because sharing insights between people can build lifelong respect.

Break bad habits

One of my great frustrations when I taught at universities in large lecture theatres was that everyone sat in the same seat every week. Think about it: you can learn only so much from the person next to you. So, in every setting you find yourself in from this day forth, sit next to someone different and see how much more you learn.

DON'T FORGET

To get the most from the insights available in your life, remember these tips:

- valuable insights can come from the most unexpected people and places
- consistently listen and observe
- make a note of the insights that have inspired you—these may help you form your own
- be curious—talk to people.

Get ahead of the pack

Here's how to really take advantage of the insights you gather:

- *Find out more:* New ideas are created every day and in some very interesting places. As an exercise, go to well-known company websites and read about the founders and the reasons they established the business. They often provide very simple and interesting insights.

- *Do it:* Remember, necessity is the mother of invention. If you think you have a great idea for a product or service, a good litmus test is to ask yourself if people really need it. Test that by giving someone you know in business a brief business plan explaining how you'd execute your idea. Testing their insight will be very valuable to you.

Meet the mentee: Shane Prasad

Shane Prasad was completing the first year of his Commerce and Global Studies degree at Australian Catholic University when he decided that he wanted to pursue his lifelong dream—to work in the aviation industry.

'I love going to the airport and could sit there for hours looking at the planes take off and land,' said Shane. 'People there are always excited. The fact that so many different cultures from around the world come together at the airport excites me. Planes allow us to visit our loved ones and to explore the world. I want to be a part of this industry that allows people to go wherever their hearts desire.'

The problem, however, was that he had no idea where to start. How could he get a foot in the door of such a highly competitive profession?

Shane visited The Naked CEO website to seek advice by asking Alex a question. Alex responded with a personal video answer that encouraged Shane to immerse himself in the aviation world. Alex advised Shane to seek out aviation-focused hobby groups that attract people who are passionate about aviation as well as people who work in the industry. This would provide insights into the industry and also help him to build relationships with key people in the sector. Alex also encouraged Shane to write a personal letter to the major airlines, offering his voluntary service.

'Offering to volunteer in particular areas is generally well received, and people want to teach you things, they want to nurture and mentor,' said Alex. 'So your job is to get in there and to start talking to people in that world and things will flow from that.'

Since receiving Alex's advice, Shane transferred into the university course of his dreams—Aviation Management at the University of New South Wales. To augment his studies, he has also joined the Australian division of the Royal Aeronautical Society, where he networks with other passionate people. What is most pleasing to Alex is that he has also applied to be a student mentor at his university in the hope of developing some new leadership skills.

Shane says that the next step in his career path is to gain industry experience through internships while he completes his degree, so he can gain an understanding of how the basic operations of an airline function. Shane plans to apply for a graduate program at either Qantas or Virgin Airlines once he finishes his degree.

'Alex told me that if I want something, it's up to me to get out there and find the opportunities available. My dream is to be a leader in the aviation industry, so from now on I'll just be working up to that and grabbing any opportunities with both hands,' Shane said.

CHAPTER 5

THE BLACK BOX

Self-confidence comes from your own journey and the successes you have experienced along the way. However, in work and life, people will either intentionally or subconsciously undermine your confidence. They may consistently criticise your ideas, for instance, or talk behind your back.

This is a harsh reality that you need to be prepared for. I learnt early on in my life and career that shielding your confidence is everything. Without confidence, you can't live, you can't feel: you must defend it. I have developed a great technique for this.

You may have heard of the black box on an aeroplane. If not, it is the piece of technology on a plane that records and protects precious data about the plane's in-flight performance. In my mind, I have built a black box that represents the same concept. But the precious data my black box records and protects is my confidence. I take the feelings of confidence and pride from my successes, put them in my black box, lock the lid and hide the key.

As you keep opening the black box and filling it with confidence, know this store of self-confidence does not make you perfect, but it does keep you strong. And it ensures the confidence about your past achievements isn't diminished when, perhaps, you make a mistake, or are confronted by someone who wants to take an axe to your self-assurance.

Everyone in their life is entitled to their confidence, so start building your black box today. Keep it protected. Draw on it.

And never let anyone or any circumstance take it away from you. It will make your self-belief unshakeable.

MAKE IT HAPPEN: HOW TO BUILD SELF-CONFIDENCE

Here are some tips for building and protecting your black box.

Think positively

At times, you may tend to have a dialogue that runs in your head that tells you things are too hard, or that you're doing something wrong. Whenever those negative thoughts start to take hold, it is important to consciously turn them around and replace them with positive perspectives.

You need to build a habit of maintaining positive thoughts. But how do you do this? Like anything else, it takes practice. These days, it is nearly impossible for me to hold negative thoughts for more than a few fleeting seconds as I have disciplined my mind to spit them out.

Start practising your rejection of negative thoughts now.

Act positively

The follow-on from disciplining your mind is to start focusing on actions. These actions are varied but include learning to smile when you don't feel like doing so, being a positive voice during a difficult meeting, providing a constructive word to a colleague who is facing difficulty, and being gracious in defeat.

Take risks

Be open to new activities and don't be afraid to take calculated risks. Many inherently try to avoid risk. But the right risk, with the appropriate safety net to protect you, can be an eye-opening experience. Think about an activity that you have always wanted to do but have avoided because you fear it could be embarrassing. Now clear your mind and give it a go.

Find the lighter side

When I know others are about to laugh at me because of some crazy thing I've done, I always find it useful to get in first. In truth, given the nature and rigours of life, it seems inconceivable that people seem to take themselves so seriously. It was clear to me from a young age that we have one short life and that we should embrace it, enjoy it and never take ourselves so seriously that we can't laugh everyday—even if sometimes it is about ourselves.

Package your past experience

Don't wait until you're preparing your next résumé to package up your past experience. Every year, summarise your key positive experiences and achievements for the year and write them down—take the pride this activity elicits and lock it inside your black box.

Next time you face adversity, remember the confidence you have accumulated and earned is yours and yours only. No-one can take it away.

For many, particularly early in their career, fear of the unknown can undermine confidence. By learning from past experience, you can come to know what issues may trigger a level of concern. For example, it might be meeting and working with new people, or presenting to an important audience. Every time you confront your fear, see it as an opportunity to overcome it and do better than you did last time. Make it a positive internal competition with yourself, and use that pride you have earned to help you.

Remember that feeling on your first day of school or university, where you were worried about finding the right classroom or lecture hall? You found it, didn't you? So, rather than having sleepless nights into the future, remember you have overcome past worries since childhood, and the outcomes of the challenges you encounter in the workplace will be no different if you maintain the right attitude.

> ### Quotable quote from Alex
>
> I learnt early on in my life and career that shielding your confidence is everything. Without confidence, you can't live, you can't feel: you must defend it.

Remember knowledge is empowering

A lack of knowledge in a work environment can challenge anyone. This may sound simplistic, but knowledge is incredibly empowering. If you have ever visited a foreign country, for instance, you will know how much more comfortable you feel if you can speak a few words of the local language.

I always apply the 'context test' whenever I feel I'm not on top of a subject. This involves a curious investigation into topics and issues around the matter, which provides me with a guide or framework that will better inform me. Train yourself to a have a curious and investigative mind.

Maintain momentum

When I'm watching sport and someone is achieving great things, the commentator often says: 'that player is on a roll.' It always reminds me that life is about a momentum of confidence built on hard work and regular achievement. That is why when students, for example, ask me how long should they stay in a particular job, my answer is simple: as long as it takes to be respected by your peers and to have mastered the role. Having positively contributed to a job, you will have a sense of completion, and that is when you are ready for the next challenge. That creates a positive momentum leading into your next role.

Avoid procrastination

It has amazed me throughout my life how small things can become insurmountable. At the core of this lies the big enemy—procrastination. Whether it is indecision about an issue, deferring a tough decision, avoiding a conversation or just being lazy, all of these things sap confidence at a rate unparalleled. People have lived to regret decisions they should have made decades before. Do not let that be you. When you recognise you are procrastinating on an issue, at the very least, speak to someone you respect, and push yourself to just do it.

Be grateful

One of the most effective ways to build self-confidence is to focus on what you have. Look around at your life and take stock of what is good, what is right and what is successful. And be thankful. Noticing and appreciating these things, valuing them as important, and noting your own contribution to having them in your life will help build your confidence.

DON'T FORGET

Remember these main ways to build your self-confidence:

- never let go of the self-confidence your achievements create
- let your achievements develop a positive and lasting momentum
- possess a curious and open mind—knowledge comes from experience
- stay positive and don't take yourself too seriously.

Get ahead of the pack

Use these tips to really build and protect your self-confidence:

- *Do it:* Thrust yourself into as many public speaking opportunities as you can. No skill is better than being able to think on your feet and address a room full of people.
- *Find out more:* Visit psychologytoday.com and search for articles on self-confidence. Knowledge is power.

Meet the mentee: Ashleigh Phegan

Ashleigh Phegan was apprehensive about commencing her degree at the University of Adelaide after a long break from the formal education environment (while she completed her high school studies via correspondence in America, followed by a gap year).

'I went into my university experience thinking, How am I going to do this? How am I going to wrap my head around this? I can't do it,' said Ashleigh.

She raised her concerns with Alex, who explained that 'success' is more than just a title allocated to a person—it is a confidence in oneself.

Alex encouraged Ashleigh to hold on to the many achievements she would experience throughout her journey, no matter how small they seemed, because doing so would ultimately help her build confidence.

'Alex told me to "lock up" any successes in my own internal "black box" and to know that even though some of your successes may be minor in the scheme of things, they can still motivate you to move forward in everything that you do,' Ashleigh said.

'The fact that the CEO of an international organisation could relate to my experience helped me to think, okay, it's normal to have these doubts. It's not just me. I can overcome this mindset.'

Ashleigh credits Alex's advice with helping her to store up enough confidence and courage to apply for undergraduate work experience with PwC midway through her degree. She is now a member of its 2014 vacation program.

Ashleigh also attended an event where she impressed a senior member of the PwC auditing team so much with her attitude that he invited her to work in the assurance team.

'This means moving my work experience program from December to July—which is a really valuable time to do work with an accounting firm because it is the end of the financial year and there is so much more going on,' said Ashleigh.

Ashleigh reflects on Alex's advice every day when she thinks about the tasks she needs to complete. She reminds herself to 'chip away' at small challenges as they come her way, which helps her to avoid becoming overwhelmed by bigger goals.

'I look back on my journey so far and say, "Look how far I've come". I've gone from being this nervous student to achieving considerable success, including gaining work experience at one of the Big 4 accounting firms. All because I asked Alex one question.'

PART II
CREATE YOUR OWN UNIVERSE

When I was a child, if ever things were difficult at home, such as when my mum's health was particularly bad, I would escape into my own universe. I would think in positive ways, creating in my mind's eye pictures and scenarios about the future and the things I wanted to achieve in my life. This process transported me to far happier places and was the beginning of what would become a lifelong habit that I call on when faced with adversity.

I believe it is important to continually think about the sort of universe you want to live in and how you are going to create it. It is a state of mind that has benefited me greatly throughout my life.

From a career perspective, creating your own universe is about stamping your uniqueness on an organisation in order to enhance its operations, which will naturally and fairly progress your career. Applying your personality, imagination and vision to a role will challenge the status quo, and that is exactly what you want to be doing. These qualities are your own—they are unable to be copied by anyone else—and by applying them to your job you will create a value that no-one else has seen before, or could have ever predicted.

By doing this, people who previously defined your role in one dismissive sentence, will likely begin to realise that you are moulding it into something much more significant, different from what they have seen before, because of the personality, imagination and vision you have invested into it. You will stand out from your colleagues.

Undoubtedly, creating your universe requires some small first steps while you're still learning to navigate professional environments and various personalities. As you might imagine, a young person who persistently trumpets new ways of doing things and challenges the status quo, like I did, does not always sit well with more experienced colleagues. In my early years, I was often collared and pulled back into line by someone more senior than me. For the sake of keeping my job, I realised I needed to be much more selective and sensitive to others when it came to creating my universe. I needed to be smarter about it. This meant creating my universe took me longer than anticipated and, at times, I felt like a wound-up doll that was bouncing off the same wall.

So, eventually, I learnt to release my foot from the accelerator just a little bit, but I never lost my curiosity. My mind continued to whir with ideas and possibilities around the world I would create if I had the authority to do so. Constantly I would ask myself, 'Why are processes the way they are? Would a different approach improve specific operations? How could we engage with customers differently? If I were "the leader", what would my approach look like?' This insatiable curiosity swelled during my first few years in the workforce, so by the time I had ascended into leadership roles where I was able to effect change, my universe was ready for creation.

That is when I faced a new challenge: getting people to believe that a new universe was worth creating.

In every new leadership role I set about planting the seeds of new ideas early in my tenure by saying to colleagues, 'Most of the world responds to the universe; I want to create it. I'm lonely, come and join me'. It is never surprising when this is met with puzzled expressions, but what I like about this statement is that it challenges compliant thinking, and tells colleagues who I am and who they might be. It also lets them know that I am expecting more than a traditional approach to doing business. What I convey is the beginnings of a vision for the business, the culture we can create and the exciting collective journey that I want to offer. Inspiring a new direction really does require the self-belief of many.

Leaders often talk about having a team of people with a particular skills mix. I also look to create the right personality mix. So I ask myself, who am I living with in my team? What do they like doing on weekends? What are their passions? Do they have a borderless mind? How do they respond to crisis? Do they have the courage to fail? Do they have real energy? Do they have initiative? My role is to ensure that across the team, I have the mix of personality types to deal with any conceivable circumstance—that way, there will always be someone with the characteristics to step up and lead in any particular situation that might arise.

On your professional journey, remember that while your core skills are very important, many others will have them also. Your personality traits are your unique selling point. So, if I'm interviewing someone for a job, for instance, I will not accept they have initiative just because they tell me they have it. I expect them to show me examples that provide evidence of it.

Interestingly, whenever I hear someone philosophising about impressive people and what they have achieved in their life, I will often hear them say, 'That person has an aura about them'. I think that is an interesting concept because, to me, what they are really saying is someone has successfully created their own universe and has become known for it. They have created an energy that excites and motivates people and precedes them before they walk into a room. Successfully creating their own universe and own way of doing things has made them who they are—therefore, we recognise they have an energy about them and they interest us.

If you want to achieve that sort of perception and reputation in the minds of others, the core requirement is being who you are, and following your passion, imagination and vision. Always follow that star ahead of you that says 'go this way'—you will be on your way to creating your own universe.

CHAPTER 6

STUDY — FINISH WHAT YOU START

After twenty years working as a university lecturer, I can't count how many times students have asked me about how they can succeed in their studies and plan for the future.

What I tell them can be categorised into four themes.

SELECT CAREFULLY

Moving from school to higher education is a significant adjustment—don't underestimate it. One of the realities of young adult life is that you're thrust into a situation where you must decide which study program to enrol in. A reasonable possibility will always exist that the program you commence may not feel like it is fulfilling your expectations, or simply does not interest you. Before taking any action to change, you need to ensure that you have tested that proposition. Speaking with your teachers, family or friends can often help you with this. Remember, however, that all courses will have areas of content that don't interest you—this does not necessarily mean the program is not relevant to your needs.

If you have concluded that the course you've selected isn't right for you and decide to change your program, ensure that you reflect on the alternative's relevance to employment. Think whether you have a more obvious interest in the topics, or if another alternative is possible that you haven't considered.

A good idea is to voluntarily sit in on lectures in other courses early on in your studies to gain both context and comparison. This process can be relaxed and could encourage you to open your mind to other study options that may more closely interest you.

FINISH—CREATE THE RIGHT MOMENTUM

My single best advice after all of my years of being involved in higher education is to finish what you start. In a perfect world, that means complete the course you have selected and celebrate your success.

In the event that, for whatever reason, you intend to drop out of a course, ensure you do so during the period that you are entitled to withdraw without failure. If that time frame has elapsed, ensure that you complete the subjects that you're enrolled in to protect your academic record. That way you will not face any obstacles if you decide to join the same or a different program at a later date.

Finishing what you start is a motto for life. Not finishing what you start can be one of the worst habits anyone can get into so don't do it. This poor habit starts by course-hopping simply because you can during your early study years. If this looks like it is happening, don't destroy your academic record; take time out, work in a dead-end job and learn how to appreciate the opportunity of study that so many in the world can't access. That's what I did and it proved a massive wake-up call.

CONSIDER EXTRA STUDY

Many graduates ask me whether they should stay at university and complete an additional qualification, or take the plunge into the full-time workforce.

To this, I can offer good news—you can't lose, whatever you decide. Either option is beneficial to your career. Listen to what your instinct is telling you and go with what you feel is right.

It is your destiny, your universe, so only you can be the master of it.

However, the rule of following your instinct has one possible exception. If you have received a formal full-time offer of employment from a relevant organisation, accepting it in order to gain invaluable workplace experience may well be worthwhile. Remember nothing is stopping you from undertaking additional studies part-time at a later date.

LEARN TO LOVE THE TERM 'STUDY'

Any discussion with a person who has achieved the success they planned will tell you that it all comes down to attitude. Your approach to the term 'study' is no different. For many years I had a terrible approach to that word. It conjured up images of imprisonment, lack of creativity and boredom. Not surprisingly, many of my results reflected that attitude.

Over time, what changed that attitude was my competitive spirit. I kept noticing that people I thought I was smarter than were getting better results than me. So, I knew that if I wanted to compete in a competitive world, I needed to view studying through a totally different lens. Once I did that, my results improved, my confidence grew and my momentum began.

MAKE IT HAPPEN: SUCCESSFUL STUDY

Here's how to take advantage of your opportunity to study, and use your studies for future success.

Be focused in your choices

At the start of your studies, anticipating which sector or even which firm you may wish to ultimately work for is always useful. The advantage of doing so is that you will focus on selecting the right elective subjects that will better improve your knowledge base and relevance for employment.

Learn to plan and prioritise

At the start of each semester, once you have received all your unit outlines, summarise on one page all the dates of the assessment requirements for the following months. Similarly, record all of your non-university commitments. Then merge both lists to ensure that no clashes with responsibilities occur. Set a plan as to how you will manage your time efficiently. This is a good habit to take into the workforce, too.

Create the right environment

Only you know the environment that you require to be productive in your studies. Some people may study listening to music, while others need a quiet, distraction-free space. No matter your choice, you need to ensure that you have a consistent place available to support your study regime. To keep stimulated, complementing this environment by occasionally working with a study group in different locations is often useful.

Understand how you learn best

It took me many years to understand how I absorbed and retained information. You need to explore the various media available to you to work out how you learn most effectively. For example, like me, you might be an auditory learner, which means that media such as podcasts, vodcasts and webinars are effective channels of communication for you. Visual learners acquire knowledge by looking at elements such as graphs and diagrams, or through watching a demonstration. Kinaesthetic learners prefer touch, such as 'hands-on' experience. Check online for supplementary resources that work in with the way you prefer to learn.

Hang in there

Having taught in large lecture theatres for many years, I am acutely aware that it is mostly a one-way process and that students need to stay focused for long periods of time. The reality is that most people have relatively short attention spans. So, it could well be that, in a two-hour lecture, you have tuned in and out multiple times, meaning in any given week you could well have missed slabs of content relevant to your final examinations. My best advice is to record your lectures, learn to take notes that summarise key issues rather than every word said, and watch any available videos or online content to complement the topics of the lecture.

Build relationships by asking questions

Teachers remember the students who try hard to be successful. They also remember the students who regularly ask questions. By getting into the habit of asking a few questions each week, you will not only hone your skills of communication, but also bring the topics to life, which should greatly assist you when articulating your answers in assessments and examinations. When you complete your studies, relationships that have been built with teachers will serve as your database for professional references on your résumé.

Quotable quote from Alex

I believe it is important to continually think about the sort of universe you want to live in and how you are going to create it...Always follow that star ahead of you that says 'go this way'—you will be on your way to creating your own universe.

Take every opportunity to gain experience

For years I witnessed students missing the opportunity to gain experience that they could record in their résumé. In higher education, these opportunities abound—but they usually need to be initiated by the student. It could be volunteering to lead a team project, speaking at an event, captaining a sporting team, establishing a club, or contributing to the university newspaper. If seeking and engaging in experience becomes a part of your mindset, your relevance for future employment—brand 'You'—will be greatly heightened.

Celebrate success

All too often in the workplace, people don't pause long enough to celebrate their successes, even though this is an important ingredient in motivation. Acknowledging your moments of success during your university career is a must, because each success builds one more layer of confidence. Remember what I wrote in chapter 5 about the 'black box'? These successful moments are the ones you should lock away inside of you forever—it will do wonders for your confidence.

DON'T FORGET

Remember these main points about studying:

- work out how you absorb information, and then play to your strengths
- learn to focus—make it a habit
- seek and engage in new experiences over and above your studies
- always finish what you start.

Get ahead of the pack

Follow these tips to really strive for success with your studies:

- *Do it:* Do you know the subjects and qualifications necessary for your dream job? If not, look at job ads and company graduate recruitment pages for examples.

- *Add it up:* Should you study more or start working after you graduate? More than 12 000 people answered the question at thenakedceo.com—check out the survey for some interesting results.

Meet the mentee: Rosalaura Annetta

When Swinburne University student Rosalaura Annetta failed two subjects, she knew it was time to make some drastic changes to her busy schedule.

'At university, we have 12 weeks each semester to learn so much, and at the start of my degree I really struggled to get on top of everything,' Rosalaura confessed. 'I couldn't fit in enough study time between socialising and working at my part-time job.'

Fortunately, Rosalaura came across Alex's study tips on The Naked CEO website. This simple study guide inspired a new and better way for her to manage her priorities—one where she felt in control, largely because she had discovered what specifically works for her.

'The tips on The Naked CEO that really stood out for me were those that focused on how to create enough time for study in a busy schedule like mine,' she said.

'When I am about to study, I now make sure I sit down and say this is what I have to do and this is how much time I have to achieve it. I then tick off what I can easily understand and focus my attention on the topics I need a bit of extra time with.'

Rosalaura's now close to achieving a distinction grade average—an achievement she never thought would be possible.

And she is now thinking even bigger, confident that applying her time-management routine to her first full-time job will help her achieve even greater success.

CHAPTER 7

NETWORKING FOR NOVICES

When I was a university lecturer, I would constantly tell my students to look around the lecture theatre and contemplate the idea that someone in there could one day become a prime minister or president, the CEO of a multinational business or a global entrepreneur. I would then ask them, 'So why are you sitting in the same seats every week, next to the same people? The future of the world is in this lecture theatre. Talk to each other and build relationships.'

While some people would respond to what I was saying, it was noticeable that others would not.

Some people feel comfortable socialising in new environments and building new relationships, whereas others do not. If you fall within the latter category, meeting new people does not come naturally to you; do not wait until you are in a work situation to resolve this. Start now, while you're still studying.

You can take small, yet effective, steps to help improve your ability and confidence as an effective communicator and networker. For instance, try saying good morning to your neighbour when you leave your house, or greet the person sitting next to you in a lecture room. The reaction you receive might not always be the desired one, but that does not matter: this exercise is about overcoming any unnecessary fears or feelings of embarrassment from an undesirable response (or no response, as the case might be).

If you persist with breaking down unnecessary barriers between you and others, it will become a habit—automatic—and it is very likely that, no matter what the professional environment or circumstance that you enter, you will possess a base confidence when it comes to meeting and interacting with new people.

When you enter the workforce and attend a professional networking event, nothing is more important than showing a genuine interest in the person you're speaking to. With numerous people in the room it can be easy to get distracted by surrounding conversations, or when you notice someone else you really want to talk to. Instead, listen and show genuine interest in the person you are in conversation with and avoid glancing over their shoulder every few seconds. You never know, in a few years' time the person in front of you now might be the person you are seeking out in the room. The best things I have ever gained in my career have come from listening.

It is important to understand that networking is not about conversing with someone because you want to get something from them, like a business or career opportunity. Great networkers don't build relationships to take, they build them to give. For instance, the person you're speaking with might detail an issue they're confronted with and you might know someone who can help them solve it. If you do, introduce them to that person. In the fullness of time, this selfless approach will likely be reciprocated. Make giving your primary focus and people will likely remember and respect you for it: this is a key to building relationships and a mutually beneficial network.

MAKE IT HAPPEN: HOW TO NETWORK

Opportunities to build your network are everywhere. It might be via social media, which I will cover in the next chapter, or it might be in a face-to-face, traditional sense with a fellow student, teacher or friend. Building and maintaining a healthy network is important for your career now and into the future.

Understand contacts may be closer than you think

Think about the people you already know. They will have parents, friends or neighbours that are likely to be respected professionals in a range of fields. Have you introduced yourself to these people? Don't presume people know about your aspirations—you need to introduce yourself and make known your career goals. I suspect you will be pleasantly surprised at how quickly suggestions come back that might help you on your way.

Get connected

I cover LinkedIn in much more detail in the next chapter, but a bit of advice regarding this social networking site is useful here. You can upload your email contacts to your account and LinkedIn will identify matches between your address book and its database. You can then use name searches to find other classmates, colleagues and professionals you want to make contact with.

To be strategic, search through your connections' connections to find interesting people you would like to get to know. Or look at your university page to seek out alumni working at companies you're interested in. Keep in mind, when inviting people to connect with you, personalising your connection requests is appropriate—do so by identifying your common ground, such as where you met or who you have worked with. You want the people in your network to know you value them and that you're not engaging them simply to boost the number of your connections. In all aspects of networking, whether physical or online, you must always maintain your authenticity.

Remember not everything happens online

To complement online interactions, investigate opportunities to attend relevant conferences, workshops or other social activities happening in your industry or in other areas of personal interest. At these events, you will meet interesting professionals with similar skills and interests that you may never have encountered in your day-to-day routine. Be brave and introduce yourself. Place yourself in new and different social settings. If you're serious about growing your network and chasing your dreams, you must take a step outside your comfort zone.

> ### *Quotable quote from Alex*
>
> If you persist with breaking down unnecessary barriers between you and others, it will become a habit—automatic—and it is very likely that, no matter what the professional environment or circumstance that you enter, you will possess a base confidence when it comes to meeting and interacting with new people.

Nerves mean it matters

Whenever someone tells me they're nervous about doing something or meeting someone new, I know it matters to them. It is important.

To live an interactive and networked life, you have to do things that matter to you. Therefore, you have to work through your unease, be courageous, and know that any nervous feelings are just your body telling you that whatever you are chasing is worth it. Embrace your nerves and don't let them steer you away from experiences.

So, whenever you are socialising and notice different reactions around the room, understand that everyone at different times feels nervous. You are not alone and, like everything in life, the more you expose yourself to situations that escalate your nerves, the more you will conquer them.

Print your own business cards

I always find it impressive when a young person looks for ways in which they might stand out from the crowd. Over the years, I have encountered an increasing number of students who have made a small investment into their own personal brand by producing their own business card. This tells me a lot about their willingness to make that extra effort. Business cards leave people with a concrete reminder of you and provide an access point should they want to make contact in the future.

Be authentic

I will keep reminding you about being authentic, as it should be at the core of your behaviour in life and at work. If the people you meet gain a sense that you are everything you appear to be, and someone to be trusted, they will likely stay in touch, help you out and introduce you to other people.

People perceive behaviour differently. When someone is overly quiet or shy, they may come across as aloof. Or when someone amps up the volume to be heard, they can be perceived as precocious or arrogant, when in fact they may be insecure. Being authentic is the best way to avoid being misunderstood. Allow your unique DNA to shine through.

If you find that being yourself is not eliciting the response you had hoped for, ask others for feedback. This feedback may sting, but if you treat it as constructive the process could be one of the most powerful steps you take towards becoming a respected and well-received professional.

Keep in mind it's not about you

As you gain more experience in your life, it will become increasingly obvious that those who spend inordinate amounts of time speaking about themselves are rarely well received. The tragedy for these people is that they are often unaware of how they are perceived, which ultimately minimises their opportunities to grow as a professional.

Your effectiveness as a networker will be strongly enhanced by being a good listener, showing a genuine interest in what others have to say, and complementing the conversations by bringing your personality gently into it. I have said it before and I will say it again: some of my most valuable career learnings have come from listening to other people's insights.

Think about the second impression

So, after meeting someone, what should you do next? A good idea is to send the person an email or, my personal favourite, a handwritten note. This is an effective way of making a lasting impression. Keep the message brief, making sure you remind them of where and when they met you, and the value you gained from the experience.

It is important not to push too hard. Like all relationships, a new professional connection is more likely to thrive if you take your time.

Remember to nurture your new professional relationships by looking for genuine opportunities to stay in touch. You have many ways to do this, such as occasionally sharing articles you see that are of mutual interest. As each new person joins your network, more potential doors to the future will open.

DON'T FORGET

Remember these main points from this chapter:

- be yourself—don't try to rush your professional relationships

- be adventurous—practise your conversation skills in all areas of your life

- disregard fear and embarrassment in all aspects of your life—what's the worst that can happen?

- be respectful and listen.

Get ahead of the pack

Here's how to ramp up your networking and make a lasting, authentic, impression:

- *Do it:* If you get nervous, or find meeting new people challenging, consider joining an organisation like toastmasters.org where you can work on your communication skills and networking ability.

- *Ask yourself:* Are you participating? Are you getting to know people at university or work? Can you name two new people you have had a good conversation with in the last month?

Meet the mentee: Patrick Taskunas

Bachelor of Business student Patrick Taskunas was eager to start building his professional network before he graduated from the University of Tasmania, but he didn't know where to begin.

After conducting some research, he came upon The Naked CEO website and asked Alex if he could be doing anything while he was still studying that would help prepare him for his chosen industry.

Alex encouraged Patrick to find opportunities to step outside of his comfort zone and develop his communication skills. In particular, he advised volunteering in a workplace or joining community groups to get to know people with similar interests. Alex also emphasised that these scenarios would help Patrick to hone his communication skills, which is key in successful networking and relationship building.

Alex said that, while on campus and in lectures, Patrick should make a point of sitting next to and interacting with different people. This would help build not only his network, but also his ability as an effective and versatile communicator.

Patrick said that this insight encouraged him to make a greater effort to speak to people, not just the people he already knew.

'I started to get to know people studying within the same faculty, and chatting to them during tutorials,' Patrick said.

It also reminded him to look into the possible networking opportunities that he had within his own family.

'It made me think about who my dad and my uncle might have in their networks,' said Patrick. 'It turns out that they actually went through university with some of the people working in senior positions at the Big 4 accounting firms in Hobart. Because of this I was able to actually get introduced and develop personal relationships with some of the leaders working within these firms.

'It made it a lot easier for me when I started applying for graduate positions, because I could ask for advice, and I felt some comfort in knowing that if I went for any interviews I might know some of the people in the room.'

Patrick has since secured a graduate position with Deloitte for 2015 and, thanks to his networking efforts at university, he already has relationships with many of the students he will be working with at Deloitte.

CHAPTER 8

GET LINKEDIN

If you have not done so already, I recommend creating a profile on LinkedIn. Having a presence on this professional social network is beneficial because it is not only a popular candidate hunting ground for recruiters, but also a worthwhile platform for exhibiting who you are as a professional.

While the reach and engagement is vast on social platforms, the principles of 'real world' networking, as I covered in the previous chapter, apply to online networking as well. You need to listen to and acknowledge individuals, communicate effectively, and respect other people's opinions even if they go against your own. Perhaps most importantly, ensure you build and maintain a reputation as a valued community member—someone who is genuinely interested in sharing ideas, offering and listening to opinions—not as someone who is in this space solely for personal gain.

Not so long ago I was invited by LinkedIn to become one of their global influencers. The role involves writing blogs about leadership and current events and interacting with other professionals. I have always loved to meet and talk to people from various walks of life, so I accepted the invitation based on the fact that it would enable me to do this on a much larger scale, albeit virtually.

As a result, I am now a part of a new community. I have met and conversed with a lot of people from all over the world, and I have reconnected with a lot of people I had lost contact with over the years. This never ceases to fascinate me. Building and maintaining your network is beneficial at all stages of your career.

Many people 'like' and 'share' the pieces I write, which I appreciate, but it is the people who take the time to offer their opinion via the comment section I enjoy the most. They are inadvertently telling me that they are curious and uninhibited about stating what they feel. I admire this mindset.

MAKE IT HAPPEN: GET LINKEDIN

Consider that every second of every day hundreds of millions of professionals are connecting in over 200 countries across the globe via LinkedIn. Due to this, I encourage you to create a presence on this platform. The following sections provide some tips.

Post your profile photo

Unlike other forms of social media, LinkedIn is a professional platform, so you need to treat it as such. Post an image of yourself that you would be happy for your boss or colleagues to see. This does not mean you need to spend money on a professional photo shoot: a plain background, a professional outfit and a friendly expression will suffice.

Position yourself with a strong headline and summary

The next step is to provide information about yourself, what you're doing now and what you plan to do in the future. This should be presented in your profile's headline and summary. If you're not sure what to write, review the profiles of professionals you respect to gain some ideas. Your headline should be five or six words and the summary a couple of paragraphs. Writing in first person is best here, but if that makes you uncomfortable, the next best option is to use bullet points. Avoid writing in third person at all costs.

Make the most of the experience you have

If you haven't started working full time yet, filling your profile may seem tough, but really it's not as difficult as you think. Many students add work experience, internships and part-time roles to this section, including committee roles at university, which is a good idea. The trick is to think about key words that translate from your early experience to the job you want in the future.

For example, if you worked in retail, you could emphasise the key sales processes and reporting mechanisms you learnt, as well as your appreciation of being a valued team player and delivering excellent customer service. You can also upload presentations, photos and videos to further illustrate your accomplishments.

Include your education

If you're currently studying or have recently completed your qualification, make sure you include these details in the education section of your profile. Also, you should add any relevant activities, participation in societies and any outstanding results you wish to share. If you have completed any other short courses or training, you can add these extra qualifications in the section called 'courses'.

Are you volunteering?

If you're trying to build up experience to get your dream job, it should go without saying that some of the best opportunities are voluntary. LinkedIn certainly thinks so—they have created a section just for volunteer experiences and causes. So even if you were not paid for a job, be sure to list it. Recruiters and employers often view volunteer experience as just as valuable as paid work. Remember to include the official name of the company you volunteered for. If they have their own company page on LinkedIn, their logo should show up against your entry.

Get endorsed

Have you noticed the skills and endorsements section on LinkedIn? This is the perfect place to start highlighting your experience and abilities using key words. You should know by now that key words are critical to recruiters when they search for candidates. Have a look at entry-level job advertisements for the key words that relate to your dream job, and add at least five of your relevant key skills so your connections can endorse you for the things you are best at.

You can also be a good connection by endorsing other people's skills. It pays not to be frivolous with your endorsements so ensure you recommend someone because they really do possess that skill, not just because they are your friend, or because you want them to endorse you in return.

Quotable quote from Alex

LinkedIn is just a microcosm of how life should work. When you're online, your approach to networking should be the same as it is when networking in person.

Promote your achievements

Your LinkedIn profile should be starting to look better populated. Now it is time to include honours and awards. Let the world know about your achievements, but keep it relevant. For example, your swimming certificate is only relevant if you have aspirations to build an aquatic career.

Add some more detail

Whether you led a group assignment at university or built an app on your own, the 'Projects' section is the perfect place to write about what you did and how you did it. If you worked with a group, don't forget to acknowledge other team members on the project.

Ask for recommendations

We all know how important recommendations are and most professional roles include a requirement to provide at least two referees on your résumé. You can also add recommendations to your LinkedIn profile and doing so will enhance your credibility relating to the strengths and skills you have highlighted. You can ask managers, professors or classmates who have worked closely with you to write a recommendation. If you receive a recommendation, you can also add additional detail by uploading relevant presentations, photos and videos.

Get connected

With your profile complete, you are ready to go, so start connecting. Join groups on relevant topics; follow companies and Influencers you are interested in. Join the conversation. Look for opportunities to stand out by adding thoughtful, relevant commentary to a discussion.

DON'T FORGET

Keep in mind these main points when connecting on LinkedIn:

- be professional in social media communities

- think carefully about your qualities and experience before posting them on your profile and connecting with others

- upload slide decks and videos to add detail

- make your profile a priority—ensure you keep it up to date with relevant activities.

Get ahead of the pack

Here's how to ramp up your activities when connecting via LinkedIn:

- *Find out more:* LinkedIn has created a whole set of resources to help students and young professionals build their best possible profile and make the most of networking via LinkedIn. Visit students.linkedin.com for more information.

- *Ask yourself:* Are you avoiding clichés on your profile? If you have claimed to be 'innovative', 'a team player' or 'highly motivated', have you given examples that evidence those traits? Too many people simply write the words and do not back them with substance.

Meet the mentee: Ash Parr

Ash Parr had a six-year career as a semi-professional poker player before, at age twenty-four, he decided on a new career direction, enrolling in a business degree at Queensland University of Technology (QUT).

It was then that Ash realised his new career course required a less casual approach in terms of how he presented himself to his peers and prospective employers. He visited The Naked CEO website where Alex emphasised that one of the most important characteristics to exhibit both online and face to face is a willingness to step out of your comfort zone and take on opportunities to learn and grow. It is about building a positive brand 'You'.

Alex's advice inspired Ash take up long-distance running, go on an international exchange to the London School of Economics and Political Science in London and actively pursue public speaking roles.

Ash also decided to set up a LinkedIn profile. He committed to regularly documenting as many relevant experiences and achievements as possible and, soon enough, his profile page was full of information that spoke volumes about his personality, initiative and determination.

'A LinkedIn profile is almost like a résumé,' Ash said. 'If it doesn't have very much on it, it doesn't tell a story, and it doesn't say anything good about you.

'Something that I've taken from The Naked CEO is that you should really invest some time into your LinkedIn profile to keep it up to date, and make sure that it looks good and that every part of it is filled out properly. As well as showing off your qualifications and your achievements, a well-maintained profile shows that you're professional, organised and reliable, and that you take pride in yourself.'

By taking on Alex's advice about how to represent himself, and using the tools available on LinkedIn, Ash feels that he has learnt a lot about developing a good personal brand.

Ash was so inspired by Alex's advice that he decided to 'pay it forward' by presenting a professional development session on personal brand in conjunction with Golden Key and the QUT Economics and Finance Society.

'It was one of the major highlights of my life,' said Ash. 'Two and a half years ago you couldn't have paid me enough money to do public speaking. The changes I made and my subsequent development is all thanks to The Naked CEO initiative. That's the value I have gained from Alex's advice.'

And when new opportunities outside his comfort zone present themselves to Ash? 'I take them on,' he said. 'If I can do public speaking, I can do these new challenges too!'

CHAPTER 9

CREATING A RÉSUMÉ THAT GETS READ

I remember this stage of my life and career very well, chiefly because most of those early memories were formed from rejection.

After I completed my Bachelor of Commerce degree, I wrote over 100 letters, with résumé attached, to various prospective employers. All of them were politely rejected or totally disregarded. But not for a second did I worry about it: they did not know me, so this could not possibly be a personal rebuke. I just presumed that I needed to write a better letter and an even better résumé. So that is what I did and, eventually, I was hired.

Although I got a lot of things wrong when I was young, I do reflect on my attitude to this situation and think that it was something I definitely got right. My persistence taught me that if you don't keep fighting for what you want, you don't really want it. It also taught me that a résumé is as much a snapshot of your background and achievements as it is of your personality. Not many job applicants focus enough on the latter, however.

Presume the recruiter has been inundated with job applications for the role that you're applying for. Going through these applications is repetitive work, so in order for you to shine out among the rest, you need to bring something different to their desktop. A lot of this comes down to simplifying your message and ensuring you're really focusing on what makes you unique and much more interesting than someone else with a similar qualification or background. Who you are as a person is your comparative advantage.

Essentially, your résumé is your one chance, in a static moment, to tell someone who you are—so it's essential to stamp your personality on it. Find ways to express your life and personality balanced with your technical skill set. It should give a recruiter a sense of the universe you have created to date and the one you hope to create with the potential employer. You want them to see that, respect that, and consequently want to open their doors and invite you in.

MAKE IT HAPPEN: CREATING A RÉSUMÉ THAT GETS READ

Reading through job advertisements is always exciting, as you imagine yourself in the perfect role and dream about all the possibilities ahead. But before hitting the 'apply' button on a recruitment website, take a moment to assess the strength of your résumé. Following a few guidelines can make a positive difference as to whether or not your résumé is read.

Your résumé is a critical step on the path towards hearing those exciting words 'you're hired!' so it is not a place to take short cuts. Commit to taking the time to create a document that you can be proud of, and ensure you review it for each role you apply for. That way you will always be putting your best foot forward.

Introduce yourself

The introduction section of your résumé is key in creating a positive curiosity in the mind of a recruiter or employer. Therefore, once you have added the standard list of personal and contact details, ensure your introduction clearly articulates your career objectives, current career status, key skills and strengths, and aspirations for the future.

If an employer likes what they read in these first few sentences, it will plant a seed of interest that will encourage them to learn more about you.

After the introduction, list your educational qualifications, including grades and institutional details. Add any additional training you have undertaken, and then move on to a reverse chronological list of your employment history, with your current or most recent role listed first, including start and end dates.

Address the key selection criteria

In many cases, job advertisements will specify key selection criteria. In the event they don't, make contact with the recruiter to see if more detailed information is available.

Deconstructing any previous experience you may have and aligning it with the criteria provided is very important. Feeling like this process is somewhat overly repetitive is normal—some activities crossover multiple criteria so it is important to maintain a keen attention to detail, avoid complacency, and have a trusted person proof your work.

Be succinct

An acceptable length for your résumé can vary according to industry, role and application criteria. However, if a word count is not stated, keeping things concise is a good rule to remember. Standard practice, particularly in the early stages of your career, is to make sure that your résumé is no more than two pages in length. This means leaving out unnecessary detail and avoiding 'rambling'. When writing your résumé, keep in mind that you are summarising your skills and experience, and that it is the interview that will provide the opportunity to furnish more detail. So keep it short and to the point.

Know what to exclude

Listing personal details such as date of birth, relationship status, or any health problems or disabilities, is unnecessary. If you have personal circumstances that may affect your ability to perform the role, you have the choice whether to state these upfront or later in the process.

Remember, while your hobbies and interests may on the surface seem irrelevant, they could provide a lot in terms of illustrating that you are a well-rounded and interesting person.

I take a particular interest as an interviewer in what makes a person who they are—what they do in their spare time helps with this.

Quotable quote from Alex

Who you are as a person is your comparative advantage. Essentially, your résumé is your one chance, in a static moment, to tell someone who you are—so it's essential to stamp your personality on it.

Avoid clichés

Drop the clichés. Keep in mind that everyone describes themselves as 'innovative', 'passionate' or 'motivated', among many other overused descriptors. Ask yourself if these predictable words could be replaced with something better. If you're going to be authentic, use your own words.

Also keep in mind that examples speak louder than words. For instance, if you describe yourself as being 'creative', illustrate this by articulating a moment or experience when this quality shone.

I know what you are thinking: I don't have the experience that allows me to provide these examples. Yes you do. Try to find parallels between your experiences at school, university or in a volunteer role with the job you're applying for. Did you lead a sports team, act as the treasurer of a club or help raise funds for a charity? You likely demonstrated or garnered useful qualities from these sorts of experiences that are applicable to a work environment—give it some thought.

Proofread your work

Lack of attention to detail has tripped up many otherwise excellent candidates. Too many of us rely on our software to pick up spelling, grammatical and punctuation mistakes but these tools are not foolproof. One mistake can send your résumé straight to the rejection pile, so it is important to check everything twice and, better still, ask a friend to proofread your résumé with fresh eyes. My view of a candidate, fairly or unfairly, is completely diminished if I note spelling or grammatical errors.

Include a cover letter, unless asked not to

In many ways, the quality of your cover letter may well determine whether your résumé is read. It should contain four brief parts.

Firstly, it should always refer to the contact person, job position and reference number (if provided) upfront. Secondly, in no more than a short paragraph, you need to explain the personal reasons the job interests you and why you are the right person. Thirdly, in a slightly longer paragraph, reference your interpretation of just the key priorities of the selection criteria and how you match them. Conclude by noting why you are interested in working for the particular organisation and reassure them of your commitment to bringing your best endeavours to the role.

Be easy to contact

Make sure your contact details are clearly listed and that you have regular access to the phone number or email address you have provided. The last thing you want is a time-poor recruiter trying to reach you on a landline when you're at university all day. Also, ensure that your email address is appropriate—no silly nicknames in your address or anything that may make you look unprofessional.

Check your online profile

Remember, many prospective employers will review all your online activities if they are serious about employing you. So, prior to applying for a job, evaluate your Facebook, Instagram, Twitter (and whatever other social network you may have a presence on) profiles, and ask yourself—would I be happy with my employer seeing this image or comment? If your answer is 'no', start deleting.

DON'T FORGET

Keep in mind these main points when preparing your résumé:

- ensure your introduction reflects your personality
- be succinct and make sure you address the key criteria outlined in the job description
- avoid clichés and use real-life examples
- have someone you trust proofread your résumé—typos are a major turn off.

Get ahead of the pack

Here's how to take your résumé building to the next level:

- *Do it:* Even if you're not currently searching for a job, update your résumé regularly with projects and achievements so you're prepared and not relying on your memory if an opportunity comes along.

- *Ask yourself:* How would you feel if you applied for your dream job but found out you had missed the cut-off date? Some job sites leave advertisements up for a set amount of time, like a month. This means that you may read an advertisement after the cut-off date, so check carefully before you invest time in preparing an application.

Meet the mentee: Damian Garthwaite

Damian Garthwaite is a Melbourne-based father of three who, in 2010, after more than ten years working in the advertising industry, made a bold decision to pursue a new career in accounting.

Within weeks of starting his Masters of Professional Accounting degree at Monash University, Damian recognised the different approach to résumé writing that people working in the accounting and finance industry took when compared with people in the advertising industry.

He knew that he would need to create a new résumé, but was not entirely sure how or what to present within it.

He sought Alex's advice.

'A really great tip that Alex gave me for creating a successful résumé was to find and speak to recruiters to find out what they're actually looking for in a good accounting résumé, and to get to know their style and apply it to my own applications', Damian said.

Damian met with a number of recruiters to obtain their feedback on his résumé. Further to that, he attended multiple information sessions and workshops held by some of the Big 4 accounting firms on how to prepare a résumé for the graduate recruitment process.

Alex also encouraged Damian to involve himself in extracurricular activities to build a strong list of associations and accomplishments for his résumé. Damian keenly followed this advice by undertaking a number of projects at Monash University, such as developing and founding the Monash Investment Society through the student union. Damian was also elected onto the university's Business and Economics Faculty Board, where he volunteered with the Monash Postgraduate Society to help international students settle in on campus.

'When I started searching for volunteer opportunities, I didn't want to take a scattered approach and sign up to do things that would appear to be "fluff" on my résumé', Damian said.

'I did things that I am interested in and passionate about, and that I would like to include in my career.'

Damian believes that this approach made his application and résumé stand out as being genuine and authentic, because any recruiter would be able to sense his passion for the activities he had been involved in.

Damian has had the opportunity to meet up with Alex in person a number of times since originally posting his question on The Naked CEO website. He says he feels as though Alex recognises that he is approaching his new career in accounting with a different set of perspectives than many other new recruits, and that Alex has provided him with welcome guidance and reassurance that he has made a good career decision.

Damian is now a consultant within PwC's Private Clients Taxation and Assurance team.

CHAPTER 10

SUCCEEDING AT JOB INTERVIEWS

Having interviewed many people at various levels of seniority, let me tell you about the scene I often witness when sitting in the interview room waiting for the applicant to enter. Two or three interviewers will be in the room, discussing who will ask which question and predicting how the candidate will answer. Typically, one of the interviewers is more senior than the other so, to some extent, and with great irony, one of the interviewers will likely be as conscious of their performance as you are of yours.

Without wanting to make you feel uneasy, I feel it is healthy for you to know that some internal politics might be at play in the room that are out of your control.

CONTROLLING WHAT YOU CAN

So, what can you control? Here are a few insights into the questions I mentally go through every time I interview someone.

Are they interesting?

My test for this is not focused on the depth of a person's ability, but the breadth of their curiosity in life. Do they have genuine outside interests? Do they have friendships spanning different backgrounds? I have often found people are more interesting than they project themselves to be. However, as an interviewer, I should not have to work hard at finding out what makes you unique.

Do they have a holistic perspective?

One of my great frustrations as a CEO are people who think solely about the position they are applying for. At the very least, I want the candidate to demonstrate an intuitive interest in the whole of the business.

Are they passionate?

It is a shut door for me if I do not recognise the applicant's emotional connection to something or someone in their life. Without passion, people simply exist, they don't live: selfishly I want to live with people, not merely exist with them. Sparks of passion are your best bet at building a pushy and positive culture—which is what an employer wants.

Are they open about their mistakes?

As I mentioned in Part I, mistakes can be your friends. The only way I have learnt anything in my career is from the mistakes I have made. In some ways, I am proud of them, but even more so I'm proud that I have learnt from them.

So anyone who in a good, healthy and open conversation claims to be mistake-free, I would prefer it if they went and worked for someone else. There is no such thing as a mistake-free person.

Do they have an opinion?

What I expect from an interviewee is a natural and comfortable perspective on significant current affairs—relevant or not to our business. Without a natural awareness of what goes on around you, how can you possibly expect to be effective in a competitive work environment?

Do they have leadership potential?

Even if I am interviewing a very young person, I look for evidence of initiative that gives me a sense of their leadership potential. This evidence might have been leading a sports team, or a new process they introduced in a part-time job.

MAKE IT HAPPEN: HOW TO SUCCEED AT JOB INTERVIEWS

If you have secured an interview with your dream employer — well done. At this stage, remember that the interviewer has already seen your résumé, they know you on paper, and so the interview is your opportunity to bring life and personality to the words.

Before you walk into the interview, remind yourself about the things that make you unique. Without overselling it, ensure your uniqueness is evident throughout the interview.

At the end of the day, interviewing a job applicant is not dissimilar to interviewing a prospective housemate. The interviewer is aware that they are going to spend a lot of time under the same roof as this person, no matter what the nature of the role. Accordingly, they're looking for a confidence that you will fit in with the other housemates, you're all that you seem, you're interesting, and you're there to make a genuine commitment.

If you look like a person who is easy to live with, you're halfway there. At the start of your career, this is much more important than your content knowledge.

I realised from a young age that, irrespective of the outcome, job interviews always provide an excellent opportunity to gain invaluable experience and learn about yourself. With this in mind, make sure you prepare, focus on doing your best and accept the employer's decision. Remember, if you are unsuccessful, there are plenty more opportunities available. Learn from the experience rather than being disheartened by it.

In the next sections, I take you through my guide to successful interviewing.

Preparing for the interview

Do your research

Preparation for an interview is not dissimilar to completing an assignment at university: your answers should be informed by your research. Thorough research will build your confidence, allowing for an intelligent and informed conversation with the interviewer.

Be a detective. Find information about the company, its history, its market presence, its brand and its competitors. If need be, practise conversations about that information with friends or parents so you become conversationally comfortable about these topics. This will also help you to be more holistic in the interview.

Glean information about the interviewers from online resources, such as Google and LinkedIn. This should give you a sense of their background, expertise, and perhaps some common ground you may share with them.

Remember, while an interview is an interaction of personalities, this sits on a foundation of research and knowledge about the employer's world.

Develop a Q&A

Before an annual general meeting, CEOs and boards prepare a list of questions they anticipate their shareholders will ask, along with answers to those questions. This is a preparation technique you can use for job interviews.

Most interviews will include standard questions such as: Why do you want to work here? What makes you the best candidate? And what do you think your strengths and weaknesses are? Think about your answers to these questions and write them down. Then pick three key messages about the characteristics you have as a person and back them with examples, such as some key achievements. Practise your answers by saying them aloud. Even better, test your answers with someone who has business experience and ask for their feedback.

The interviewer will also ask questions more relevant to their particular company and industry. Again, think about what those questions might be, and then list your best answers. The advantage of such preparation is that you're immersing yourself into the environment of that business, so even if they ask completely unexpected questions in the interview, you should still be able to draw on that preparation and have something relevant to say.

Also, I can almost guarantee you the interviewer will ask if you have any questions. Again, list your questions down and practise asking them. Make sure they have not already been answered in the job advertisement or during the interview. The next section provides more about this.

In the interview

Create a great first impression

Whether it is right or wrong, people form impressions of someone else in a matter of seconds. So, in a job interview, don't discount the significance of the first few seconds.

Arrive on time, walk with quiet confidence, extend a firm handshake, make good eye contact, use people's names, speak clearly and smile. Body language, in life, in your first job, in a CEO role, is an absolutely central ingredient of success. Little things count also. Be polite to every person you meet as soon as you enter the building precinct because people talk and share opinions.

Consider this (it happened to me): you have just walked into the prospective employer's building and at the elevator you smile and let people on before you. It could turn out that one of those people is involved in your interview, so they like you even before you walk into the interview room. How's that for a great start?

Know how to respond to 'Tell me about yourself'

I have to say, I mostly remain stunned about how poorly people—even those in the most senior roles—respond to this prompt. The interviewer will not be expecting a line-by-line description of everything you have done. Remember those three key messages you prepared earlier? This is the time to deliver them. Keep your answer brief and no more than three to four minutes.

Remember subtle and sensible promotion does not hurt

Answering questions with passion and detail is great, but you have to stop and take a breath every now and then. I have found that quite often candidates will have a tendency to talk too much in interviews. They are nervous so they ramble. Your potential boss will understand you are nervous, but they will only give you so much leeway. A good idea when you're speaking is to keep an eye on everyone's body language—it will tell if you're going on too long.

When you mention your first achievement or highlight, promote the passion around it, but be 'less is more' in content. If the interviewer asks you to elaborate, you will then develop a sense of the timing and detail they are expecting per answer.

Quotable quote from Alex

I have often found people are more interesting than they project themselves to be. However, as an interviewer, I should not have to work hard at finding out what makes you unique.

Ask if you can rephrase a response

It happens to us all—either we said something we did not mean, or we mistakenly say something without any sense of political correctness. It can happen in the workplace, it can happen at home; worst still, it can happen in an interview. If it does, remain calm, think about what you would really like to say instead, and then ask if you can rephrase that answer. Remaining calm may just impress the interviewer, demonstrating your ability to remain cool under pressure and acknowledge an error of judgement. Again, this will say a lot about your authenticity.

Be truthful if you don't know

It's a matter of fact that some questions in an interview will be easy, while others may be difficult.

I am not ashamed to tell you that, even though I am a CEO, I do not always know the answer to every question I am confronted with. If you do not understand the question, ask the interviewer to rephrase it or provide further detail. If you simply do not know the answer, admit to it. You might be worried about the consequences, but it is far worse to try to 'wing it' or be disingenuous. If it is a bit of a curly question, the interviewer will likely be more interested in how you answer. Honesty really is the best policy.

Have questions

Your Q&A preparation should stand you in good stead at this point. To impress the interviewer, ask questions in their interest, not your own. Things like: What would you like me to accomplish in the first two to three months? Or, what does a top performer look like in your team? Ask about the culture and company, or anything positive that has cropped up in your research. This will help reaffirm you as a thoughtful, mature candidate.

If you're worried that you do not know enough about the job, conditions or salary on offer, ask the interviewer if they can provide an overview of the role, expectations and environment—just do not make this your first or last question.

Interviewers are always additionally impressed if you can demonstrate an awareness of matters of national interest. You can do this during the question time. During the research phase, you would have (or should have), scanned the news for anything happening in the world that may have a bearing on their business. This knowledge can make for an ideal lead-in to a question—for example, 'I read the other day that some companies are still struggling to recover from the global financial crisis—how has your business fared?'

After the interview

Make contact with your interviewer a day or so after the meeting and let them know you enjoyed the meeting and appreciated the time you were afforded. This is also your opportunity to follow up with any further details on information you provided during your interview, including things like references, portfolios or examples of your work and qualifications.

At the very least, a follow-up email will ensure that your interviewer knows you are excited about the prospective role, and that you're a considerate communicator. A handwritten note will really make you stand out. And if any questions in the interview stumped you, making contact is a great way to demonstrate a persistent interest in the job, and may impress some interviewers by showing you follow up and want to learn.

DON'T FORGET

Remember these main interviewing tips:

- research the business and the people who are interviewing you
- arm yourself with three key messages about the characteristics you have as a person, and back them with examples
- consider every first impression—listen, smile, use names
- don't be disheartened if you don't get the job—keep your head high and learn from the experience.

Get ahead of the pack

Here are some ways to really get the most out of the interview process:

- *Do it:* Most companies will have established pages on LinkedIn, Facebook, Twitter, Instagram and more. Links for their pages on these social networking sites are often found on the home page of their website, so if you are about to be interviewed, follow first. You would be surprised how many people will check to see if you are following them on social media.

- *Ask yourself:* In interviews do you answer the question asked or the one you wanted to be asked? Listen carefully and always make sure you relate your experience to the job you are applying for, particularly if your past experience is different to this position.

Meet the mentee: Kevin Singh

Kevin Singh is in the final year of a Bachelor of Commerce degree at the University of Melbourne. With dreams of one day becoming the chief operating officer of a multinational firm, Kevin knows an important first step on the journey is successfully attaining a graduate role.

He approached Alex for some guidance on interviewing for his first corporate position. Of particular interest to Kevin was advice on how to be himself in a job interview, while at the same time presenting himself as the kind of person that a company might be specifically looking for.

Alex emphasised the importance of being yourself and authentic, over trying to mould your personality to fit a specific business or job description.

'Basing my responses to questions on my own ideas helps me to participate in a conversation far more easily than if I were to try to give an answer that I think "the ideal candidate" might give,' Kevin said.

'Alex said when you go into an interview, be proud of who you are and of your achievements, and share the best version of your true self.'

Alex also recommended that Kevin research the employer and learn as much as possible about the role. Rather than reciting facts about the company, he encouraged Kevin to show his understanding of the role and industry through relating them to his own experiences and aspirations.

'I've worked hard,' Kevin said. 'I have a lot of experiences under my belt and my résumé is good for someone my age. So Alex's advice inspired me to just go with what I have so far and to be proud of that.'

In the past Kevin had tried pre-empting what employers might want to hear during interviews, but when he took Alex's advice on board he said that he felt as though he had significantly increased levels of confidence, because he wasn't trying to pretend to be someone else. As a result he was able to focus on giving clear and honest answers based on his own knowledge, understanding and experience, and, ultimately, to secure the graduate job that will kickstart his career.

Kevin recently secured a graduate role at GE, commencing in 2015.

PART III
IT'S ALL ABOUT THE PEOPLE

When I was a young university lecturer, every day I would arrive in the lecture theatre where 500 restless students and a floor littered with paper planes would be waiting. The lecture the students had just sat through obviously had not captured their full attention. Many were beyond bored and now they had to sit through another hour of lessons, this time with me at the front of the room. Rather than feeling intimidated by this seemingly tough crowd, I commenced every lesson with a tremendous feeling of appreciation.

Why, you may ask?

Because the students were not the only ones who were learning something. Every day I stood at the front of that theatre, I knew I was gaining and honing priceless skills in how to communicate effectively with people from various walks of life. This was my communication boot camp. If I could successfully encourage restless students to consistently engage and stay with me during a lesson, I could transport that skill to anywhere in my working life.

It was not long before I worked out the two fundamental qualities a person must possess in order to be an effective communicator: you must be a keen listener and a keen observer. Let me illustrate this for you. When I entered the lecture theatre I would immediately notice the students' 1000-mile stares and slumped body language. As I organised myself on stage, I would briefly hear snippets of their conversations with one another, which usually included things like, 'I need the weekend', 'Can I copy your notes?', 'Let's go out tonight'. Rather than ignoring this situation and sticking to a script like some might, I used what I saw and heard to enlighten my approach. Their minds were obviously somewhere outside of the theatre, so I needed to earn their attention with a high-energy approach. I would often move around, walk up the aisles between the seats, sometimes sit among the students, and add humour with what my children would probably call 'Dad jokes'.

Combining these rather unorthodox approaches helped me disturb any boredom-induced comas. I was able to build a genuine rapport by listening to, observing and engaging the students in a way they related to. I am proud to say that in my almost twenty-year teaching career, I never had a paper plane take flight in my class.

Listening and observing are disciplines I practise to this day. For example, if I am speaking to a group of managers, I am also furiously looking around that room and absorbing everyone's body language. By doing this, I can identify if what I am saying, the messages I am articulating, are actually having the desired effect. If they are not, I will either change the subject, move differently, or I will call a break to the meeting. Seriously, it is a waste of time to go on if people are obviously not engaged. I am always stunned when I see experienced people continue to communicate when clearly no-one is listening. They waste so much energy trying to force their messages on people. Frustration inevitably sets in on all sides, with material impacts on cooperation and productivity.

To me, people who continue on like this have not read the tone of the room and adapted their communication to a style that will work for that particular audience. They have not listened and observed.

Remember, when you're entering a new job, you're stepping into a pre-made environment that has likely existed for a long time. The people there will already feel at ease, whereas it will likely take you time to relax. This is why the first few days, weeks, even months, are all about testing the water in terms of the people you are working with. In the workplace, fools really do rush in. Take your time and be sure to test your communication skills with the people around you. Observe their behaviour and body language, and the types of people they react well to and the ones they do not. Listen. How does a particular individual relay or respond to direction? Are they short and to the point, or do they like to take their time and chat about other things in the process? In your immediate team, these are things you should try to identify early on because doing so will help you build rapport and respect.

Some graduates are at a bit of a disadvantage when they arrive in the professional world. This is because higher education study programs, while very good, are focused on content knowledge. It is perhaps not surprising, then, that new recruits often spend too much time and energy trying to promote their knowledge. While content knowledge is important, I can't emphasise enough that success in the workplace is about how you interact and live with people. The earlier you understand that life is about people and relationships, the quicker you will get on the journey that matters. It is important that you learn how to like being with people and how to glean the best of who they are. Start working on this early on in your career and you will be on a great trajectory towards becoming an empathetic and respectful leader.

Not everyone will react the same to you. Some might be open and inviting, eager to get to know you, whereas others might be a bit more aloof, more interested in getting on with their work. When experiencing the latter, do not take it personally. You may not have received your desired response for a multitude of reasons. It could be that the person is distracted by a tight deadline, they could have personal issues on their mind, or they may simply be shy. Over time you will start to work out why they respond the way they do so you can refine how you communicate with them. It is not about changing who you are, but about refining certain aspects of how you communicate or behave.

I would say to any person, at any age, that if your communication skills are not great, make it a priority in your life to improve them as soon as possible. I really mean that. An effective communicator is often the solution to issues in the workplace. An ineffective communicator can often be the catalyst for a mistake or problem. You can improve your communication in multiple ways but, like most things in life, it comes from practice. I have known professional people who talk to their reflection in the mirror at home before embarking on a negotiation or meeting someone important. This might sound a bit silly, but this exercise will show you a lot about your delivery and body language—for instance, your body language may contradict your verbal message. If I am slumped back in my chair during a meeting, this will likely send the message that I am uninterested even though I believe I am totally engaged and making a positive point.

During the first few days and weeks in a job, your boss or manager will be observing whether you're easy to work with and good company to be around. I can't stress enough how important it is to avoid being perceived as someone who is difficult—for example, someone who comes across as a 'know it all' or unmotivated, or someone who does not listen. If your bosses observe these sorts of behaviours, or someone else raises it with them, valuable time will need to be spent addressing it with you and this is not a great situation to be in.

CHAPTER 11

THE FIRST DAY
OF A NEW JOB

I vividly remember day one of my first full-time job. Brimming with an inflated ego, nervous with anticipation and eagerness to impress, I entered the foyer of the building on Sydney's Hunter Street, each step towards the elevators sending me deeper into the great unknown. Nameless faces were everywhere, all of whom seemed so comfortable in one another's company. Quickly I began to feel like an outsider, alone, and this unpleasant feeling stayed with me throughout the day. So much for the inflated ego!

I have come to learn that those feelings were completely unnecessary. Here is why. Everyone would have known, given my fresh face and brand new suit, that my knowledge and experience levels could not have been substantive. Therefore, their expectations of me would have been far less than those that I had for myself.

Day one for you is unlikely to involve questions about your content knowledge. They're not expecting you to dazzle them with what you learnt at university. They don't want you to pose myriad questions just because you think you should. If you hear or observe something that looks particularly relevant or interesting, then ask a question.

Also, this will be a day that you will never forget, so why not focus on making it a positive memory? Know that any feelings of being an outsider will dissipate. Remember how you felt when you first arrived on campus? The people were different, you did not know where the lecture theatres were, everything was probably bigger and busier, but you adapted over time, right? This is exactly what will happen in the workplace.

On your first day, your manager will likely introduce you to the key colleagues you will be working with. Remember what I wrote about first impressions in chapter 10? That is right: be respectful, be polite, but most importantly, just be yourself. That should be your focus during introductions. Doing this from day one will set you on a positive path in the minds of your colleagues.

Meeting new people can feel like you are in a whirlwind. It is likely you will struggle to remember everyone's name, so, wherever possible, write down their name and title after you have spoken to them. Then, before the day is out, try to go past at least half of those you have met and say hello to them by name. Over the first week, try to master as many names as you can.

What your employer will expect of you during the first few days and weeks is an ability and keenness to absorb information, and to start establishing relationships with your colleagues. Be conscious of how many and what questions you ask, because sometimes you can be so nervous that you ask questions about everything. Normally you will be given content to read to help with your initial understanding of the business, so don't spend a lot of time asking a multitude of questions, just try to absorb. Make notes about what you want to ask, sleep on them, and you may find four questions have become one. Remember, the people around you will be busy, so be respectful of their time and pick your moments wisely. For instance, when your manager is rushing to a meeting it is not the time to ask a question.

MAKE IT HAPPEN: SURVIVING YOUR FIRST DAY AT A NEW JOB

The following sections provide some tips to making a great first impression at your new job.

Work out what to wear

Start with paying attention to what people in the office are wearing during your interview. If you can see a mix of corporate and casual wear, always err on the side of formality because it is always better to overdress than underdress. You will be much better informed for day two.

Be early or on time

If you're using public transport, make sure you test the duration of the trip prior to your first day—preferably on a weekday. Also, be prepared for an unexpected disruption: have a taxi company number saved on your phone and money handy should you quickly need an alternative mode of transport.

Make a great impression

Great impressions come from your ability to listen and observe. Be polite and respectful to everyone you meet. Look for opportunities to exhibit your willingness to help a colleague or a team on your first day. Be consistent with these behaviours from this day forth.

Be confident

Never lose sight of the fact that this day will be regarded forever as an exciting and formative moment of your life. Treat it with the confidence it deserves. Take the day's events in your stride. The first day of a job is one of life's true character-building experiences, so focus on being yourself and just enjoy it.

Be friendly

Always be pleasant and work to be known as the friendly new recruit. However, you will not know the culture in your new workplace, so ensure you behave like a mature professional. Until you really understand your colleagues, behave around them in the same way you did during your interview process. Resist being overly familiar even if others are.

Quotable quote from Alex

The earlier you understand that life is about people and relationships, the quicker you will get on the journey that matters.

Think before you ask

If there is a concept that you do not understand, or a task that you do not know how to undertake, take time to think about what it is exactly that you don't understand. By doing this you will likely rationalise the issues into a smaller number of questions or themes. Then it is time to arrange a meeting with the appropriate colleague or supervisor to address these matters.

Learn as much as possible

No matter what happens in your first job, you will learn something. Maintain this mindset. Imagine yourself as a sponge absorbing everything around you—the people, the issues, the politics and the hierarchy. Take the time to review resources, socialise the issues and learn what makes people tick.

Update your social media profile

Update your LinkedIn profile to reflect the new position. This will help you to connect with other people in the business. These people will then have a better chance of getting to know more about you, even though you may have not yet met face to face.

DON'T FORGET

Remember these tips for your first day on the job:

- most importantly: arrive on time!

- enjoy it—this attitude should help settle some of those nerves

- don't be in a rush to ask too many questions—listen and observe

- be friendly to everyone you encounter—a simple smile, eye contact and 'hello' sends the right message.

Get ahead of the pack

Here's how to really make a difference on your first day in a job:

- *Add it up:* It's widely reported that most people will have between five and seven career changes in their life. This could mean starting a new job or being promoted. So remember—you may only have seven first days in your career. Build the positive mental focus that you will enjoy every moment of these rare life experiences. Such an attitude gives you your best chance to deliver the best first impression.

- *Do it:* Within the first twenty-four hours, build into your memory the key departments of the business and the names of all those around you in your day-to-day activities.

Meet the mentee: Waqas Durrani

When University of Tasmania student Waqas Durrani found out he had secured a job as client relationship manager at a financial services company, he was understandably excited.

Anxious to make a good impression on his first day, Waqas drew upon advice Alex had given him: that the way he interacted with his colleagues in a new job would set the tone for his future relationships and networks within the organisation.

'It comes down to your communication style and your ability to show people your own value', Alex had told him. 'At your stage in your career, the important thing will be not only the work you do, but also the way you conduct yourself, and the nature with which you speak to people.

'For the first few weeks of a job you should focus on getting in there and learning the job, and also making sure you learn people's names. Learn as many names as you can. And from that, you'll naturally begin conversations with people.'

So Waqas ensured he introduced himself to as many of his new colleagues as possible, repeating their names as a mark of respect and to help him remember them. He also worked out a simple, yet, effective tip: 'You have to wear a smile every day,' Waqas said. 'It's the best accessory you can have. It's something everyone can do. And it makes you seem more approachable and warm to people and they are receptive to that. They will smile and be friendly in return.'

The importance of having a good attitude towards a new job, and to focus on doing a great job each day, was also something that Alex shared with Waqas.

'When you're new to a role there's a lot to learn, and Alex taught me that my goal should always be to improve and push myself further—not to simply become successful.'

Waqas is settling in to his new role very well, and says that he feels proud to be a part of his new team. When he goes to work, he is grateful for the opportunity and he reminds himself that he was hired because people believed in him.

CHAPTER 12

ESTABLISHING A RAPPORT WITH YOUR COLLEAGUES

One of the great freedoms of being a child is that if you do not like something or someone, you can walk away. Remember what it was like in the school playground? There were those kids you never quite got on with, the ones who you avoided or ignored, and those who you really had great friendships with. To a degree, workplace dynamics between people are much like this, but a major difference is that avoiding or ignoring people is unacceptable. Unlike the playground, you need to find a fundamental way to coexist, communicate and be productive with everyone in your team.

Exhibit your natural values and promote them in a subtle way so people get to know you are an effective communicator. One of the best ways to do that is to make a point of going around the workplace and saying hello to people, very quickly—do not stay too long. Make eye contact, smile and say hello as you pass in the corridor, elevator, foyer, wherever you may be. They might not be the people you will be working with directly, but if you make an effort to be pleasant to everyone, I guarantee you that they will become advocates of you. This is because you have exhibited a positive and pleasant exterior.

With the colleagues you will be working closely with, ensure you invest time into knowing them—not just at a professional level, but a human level, too. Fairly early on you will identify the people that you have an immediate chemistry with and those you are going to have to work at. With the former, you will feel at ease and the conversation will flow naturally; as for the latter, they may come across as uninterested in developing a relationship with you. Resist any desire to shy away, avoid or, even worse, ignore these people. Striking a chord with some people can take time, or might not eventuate at all, but you need to try. It is always a learning experience.

If your relationship with someone does not organically improve over time, instinct may tell you that the person has a problem with you. If that proves to be right, think about how you might be able to modify the way you communicate with them. Perhaps they are in better spirits in the morning rather than the afternoon. Perhaps they prefer someone who arrives at their point quickly and without any chitchat. Perhaps something is going on in their personal life that is influencing the way they respond to you. Your best chance of discovering a greater truth about their behaviour is to remain respectfully curious, open-minded and non-judgemental.

Establishing a rapport with your boss is not about establishing familiarity; it is about showing your respect, and your determination to learn and work as part of a team. They are the key messages that you want to send. If your boss wants to get to know you on a deeper level, you will know this by the sorts of questions they ask you. Follow your manager's lead and, over time, you will work out how best to relate to him or her.

MAKE IT HAPPEN: HOW TO ESTABLISH RAPPORT WITH COLLEAGUES

The following sections take you through some of the best ways to build rapport with your colleague and managers.

Be part of it

Sharing conversations, meals and other celebrations can help you to build a community within a team. Take the initiative by being the one to offer to organise a lunch or afternoon tea so the team can relax and to get to know each other better. Develop the habit of being comfortable in people's company.

MY PARENTS' WEDDING DAY. MANY DREAMS, BUT MANY CHALLENGES LAY AHEAD FOR THEM. THEY INSPIRED US WITH THEIR COURAGE IN FACING ADVERSITY.

MUM LOVED THE SEA. THIS IS ONE OF MY FAVOURITE SHOTS — SHE LOOKS PEACEFUL AND HAPPY.

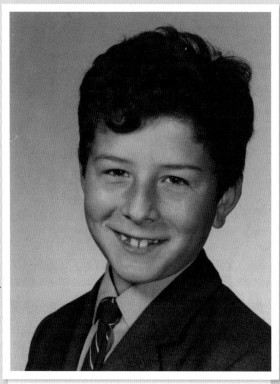

WHY DO PARENTS INSIST ON TAKING SHOCKER PHOTOS OF THEIR CHILDREN? I STILL STRUGGLE WITH TIES.

WITH MUM. THE SAFEST PLACE IN THE WORLD WHEN I WAS A BOY. MY ADVICE: APPRECIATE YOUR MUM WHILE YOU CAN.

THE GREAT MAN IN A SPORTING MOMENT, CONVINCED OF AN INTERNATIONAL CAREER. OH WELL, CAN'T WIN THEM ALL.

WHEN IN MEXICO… YES, THE MOUSTACHE WAS REAL AND YES, WHAT WAS I THINKING?

Why we employ romantics

Associate Professor Alex Malley is not your everyday accounting professor. He challenges students to think beyond accounting, and encourages them to use the profession as a stepping-stone to what they really want to do in life. He calls it "the romance of accounting" and he's inspired over 25,000 accounting students in his uniq and encouraging way. Like all of the academ ic stars at Macquarie University, Associa Professor Malley pushes the boundaries of h field. To find out more about Macqua University and its lecturers, just go www.mq.edu.au

MACQUARIE
UNIVERSITY—SYDNEY

AUSTRALIA'S INNOVATIVE UNIVERSITY

Illustration by Nigel Buchanan

I WAS ALWAYS PROUD AND GRATEFUL TO HAVE BEEN A TEACHER — IT IS MY ZEN TO SHARE TIME WITH YOUTH.

DOING WHAT I LOVE DOING, SPENDING TIME WITH STUDENTS — ON THIS DAY AT QUEENSLAND UNIVERSITY OF TECHNOLOGY.

WITH THE COOL AZRAN OSMAN-RANI, CEO OF AIR ASIA X AND STUDENT GUEST CELIA ON AN EPISODE OF THE NAKED CEO.

WITH ADAM ROSENBERG, OUR VERY TALENTED, AND FIRST, STUDENT DIARIST ON THE NAKED CEO WEBSITE.

INTERVIEWING THE VERY INTERESTING RICHARD WILKINS ON THE NINE TODAY SHOW SET WITH STUDENT GUEST EMMA-JAYE.

IN CONVERSATION WITH THE MULTI-TALENTED KATE CEBERANO ON THE BOTTOM LINE SET — WHAT A KIND AND THOUGHTFUL PERSON.

WITH STUDENT GUEST BROOKE JENNINGS AFTER HER MENTOR SESSION WITH ME ON ENHANCING HER DELEGATION ABILITIES.

WITH STUDENT GUEST WAQAS DURRANI AFTER OUR MENTOR CHAT ABOUT THE VALUE OF COMMUNICATION AND WORKING RELATIONSHIPS.

IN MY CAPACITY AS CEO OF CPA AUSTRALIA I SPOKE LIVE TO THE NATION FROM THE NATIONAL PRESS CLUB ON AUSTRALIA'S COMPETITIVE FUTURE.

A BIT OF ADVICE — WHEN YOU BECOME A CEO ALWAYS SMILE FOR THE ANNUAL REPORT PHOTO.

Show respect

Being consistently punctual for meetings demonstrates that you acknowledge other people's time is valuable. Another sign of respect is being aware of any stress or pressure your colleagues might be under, such as a tight deadline. Offer to help out where you can or give them some space if they need it. Respect should be applied in all areas of work, including using people's names and being aware of team members' cultural differences and lifestyles.

See the lighter side

You have heard it before but I will say it again because it is just that important: be yourself. If you're funny in your social life, you can likely add that value to the workplace. However, you need to be very careful about how you manage humour in a business environment. Nothing is better than laughter to bring down the invisible walls between two or more people. It is also a tried-and-tested tension diffuser. Just remember you need to earn the right to have that freedom—this will come when you've taken the time to get to know the people around you.

Quotable quote from Alex

Striking a chord with some people can take time, or might not eventuate at all, but you need to try. It is always a learning experience.

Find common interests

Relating to someone who has things in common with you, such as attending the same high school, or knowing a common person, is easier than relating to someone you don't know anything about. If you have something in common with the other person, don't be shy in pointing it out, because it can be a good icebreaker.

Take note of your posture

When speaking with your colleagues, be conscious about your posture and body language. Ensure that they complement the tone or circumstance of the conversation.

Understand it's not about you

When you meet someone, focus more on their life than yours. Listening carefully to what they have to say will very quickly allow you to find areas of common interest. You will discover that people remember those who showed a genuine interest in them.

Reward a victory

All too often the world does not recognise or reward great effort. To one day be a great leader, you will need to make this part of your personal culture. So start now. If someone at work has achieved a milestone, make a point of going out of your way to congratulate them, whether they are in your team or not. People respond well to and always remember genuine positive reinforcement.

Build relationships

At the core of your survival and success is your capacity to build effective relationships that are equal in terms of respect and willingness to cooperate. At times, you will need to ask someone for assistance. In turn, the person who helped you will expect you to be equally supportive in reverse circumstances. These relationships must be built on an honest and mutual rapport over a period of time. Be patient: most good relationships take time. Avoid building relationships simply for possible future advantage because it will not bring out the best in either party.

Avoid office politics

One of the great challenges in early career life is recognising office politics, let alone understanding it. One of the many advantages of being a good communicator is that it may open your mind to the existence of politics all around you. Work to stay out of office politics, but always seek to understand it.

DON'T FORGET

Here are the key points to building rapport in the workplace:

- be patient—developing quality rapport with your colleagues takes time

- be genuinely interested in what colleagues have to say

- be careful—your body language speaks louder than words

- observe behaviour—get to know your colleagues and be curious.

Get ahead of the pack

Want to take your rapport building to the next level? Here's how:

- *Do it:* Strike up a conversation with a person you haven't met in the office. Find out about that person, whether you have any common interests and what they actually do in the business. You could meet a new work friend.

- *Ask yourself:* Do you have trouble initiating a conversation with people at work? If you do, consider three questions that might encourage conversation. These could relate to the weekend, school ties or hobbies.

Meet the mentee: Christina Li

When Christina moved from China to Australia her limited confidence in the English language made her concerned about developing professional relationships and communicating.

Christina conveyed her feelings of apprehension to Alex. It was then that Alex taught Christina the true value of establishing a rapport with others. He encouraged her to take chances by chatting to as many people as she could to build her confidence and learn to communicate with others in order to establish a rapport with them.

Christina reflects that, when she met Alex, she did not expect him to give her as much time and advice as he did.

'It was a surprise for me, because I was so shy and I had viewed Alex as someone who was so much more important than me. But interacting with a CEO gave me confidence. Alex's down-to-earth attitude made me realise I should not be scared to talk to others in senior management positions,' Christina said.

'Alex gave me some really inspirational advice. At the core of it was the concept that because I'm still so young I have nothing to lose, and so whenever I see an opportunity to talk with someone new, I should just be brave and put myself out there. And not be afraid of rejection.

'I just keep starting conversations with as many people as I can. I've learnt that most people want to get to know you and to help you, and this has encouraged me to be brave and express myself.'

After their discussion, Christina ran for the role of international student officer in the University of Adelaide Student Representative Council. After the elections, she secured not one, but two positions—international student officer, and board director for the Adelaide University Union. She has also gained a role in an accounting firm, where she builds relationships with colleagues and clients on a day-to-day basis.

Christina says that some of these clients are much more senior, but she now knows that she has the ability to develop a professional relationship with anyone.

CHAPTER 13

REMEMBERING AND USING PEOPLE'S NAMES

Nothing is more impactful in a conversation than referring to someone by his or her name. If someone says, 'Hello, Alex, my name is...', they have got my immediate attention and they have already impressed me.

Sound obvious? Let me tell you, the number of people in the workplace who do not use or remember people's names is quite extraordinary. They have either forgotten or were never aware of how important it is during workplace interactions. It is such an effortless demonstration of respect and politeness and it should never be undervalued. I encourage you to make remembering and using people's names a habit. People have casually admitted to me that they are 'bad at remembering names'. If this person works for me, I don't hesitate to tell them that this is a weakness they need to attend to immediately.

An individual's name is more than just a label. It can reveal many fascinating stories about a person. For instance, when I meet someone with an interesting or unusual name, I will often ask about it. This frequently reveals things about the person's family heritage, their parents and where they come from—things I would not have learnt had I not asked. As I noted in chapter 12, when appropriate, asking someone about their name can be a great icebreaker and can help you get to know people on a deeper level. It is not just a discipline in politeness and respect; it really can trigger fascinating stories about someone's life.

At the start of a new job, you will have many new names to remember. I struggled with this early in my career, so I turned remembering names into a game. Every morning on the way to work I would challenge myself to remember as many names as possible that day. I would then make a point of walking past those people and referring to them by name when I said 'hello'. Their response was always positive. Not only did this help me to remember, but, albeit unwittingly, I also was building a reputation as the person who knew everyone. This reputation became part of my brand. It is quite powerful to be standing next to your boss in an elevator and, when the doors open, greeting by name three of the five people who walk in. It is an impressive ability and people will notice. You will start generating ambassadors who will promote your ability as a communicator, together with your respectfulness and friendliness.

MAKE IT HAPPEN: REMEMBERING NAMES

The following are some effective ways to make sure you remember people's names.

Listen carefully

When someone tells you their name, make a point of remembering it. For some this comes naturally, while others have to work at it. Be sure to develop a technique, such as repeating their name a few times in your head, that allows you to recall names when you need to. Make the effort to pay close attention during introductions.

Ask again

If you didn't hear a person's name correctly the first time, you need to persist and get it right at the time of introduction. Don't wait until the end of the conversation to ask again, because it will come across as though you were not taking notice of what the person was saying.

Check your interest

Showing an interest can be as simple as asking a question about a person's name, like where it originated from. If it is difficult to pronounce, repeat it aloud and don't be embarrassed if the person corrects you. They will likely appreciate that you made an effort to get it right, and it will help you to remember it next time.

Quotable quote from Alex

People have casually admitted to me that they are 'bad at remembering names'. If this person works for me, I don't hesitate to tell them that this is a weakness they need to attend to immediately.

Connect their name to a mental picture

If you can attach a mental picture to a person's name, it will be easier to recall next time you meet. Or, you can break down their name into phonetic syllables and create images that allow you to remember the association.

Ask for a business card

A business card exchange certainly assists in maintaining a record of a person's details. However, do not overly rely on them—keep refining your ability to memorise people's names and details.

Use names appropriately

I need to make this point quite clear: there is a risk of overusing someone's name. If you do, it might be considered to be forced and disingenuous. Over my career I've been the recipient of people repeating my name multiple times in one conversation. Each time this occurs my trust in them and what they're saying diminishes. So using someone's name should be a sign of respect, not a sales technique.

DON'T FORGET

Keep in mind these pointers when focusing on remembering people's names:

- make a mental note of the person's name as soon as they say it

- write down their name after you've met them

- this skill helps you to influence—work at it

- using someone's name is respectful but don't overdo it.

Get ahead of the pack

- *Find out more:* Multiple websites speak to the power of a name from a human impact perspective. It's interesting—when people argue, they often refer to each other as 'he' or 'she' rather than by name. This is their sign of disrespect. Never fall into the trap. Google 'the power of names'—the information you can find is fascinating.

- *Do it:* Observe conversations around you more closely. Compare and contrast those people who use names as a sign of respect against those who don't. See if your results match the knowledge gained from your Google research.

Meet the mentee: Tim Pitcher

With two years left of his combined Accounting and Law degree at the University of Notre Dame, Tim Pitcher was thinking about how to find opportunities to build his network and to develop the interpersonal skills that would help him to build a fulfilling career.

Tim dreams of living in New York and working in either a law or accounting firm where he can combine the skills attained through both of his degrees. He says that his ultimate career goal is to become a senior partner at a large firm.

But Tim, who currently works part-time and studies in the Australian coastal city of Fremantle, acknowledged that although his university qualifications would provide him with the technical skills he needed to achieve his goals, he also needs to spend the coming years developing a strong set of soft skills like communication and team building.

Alex spoke with Tim about many aspects of social interactions in the business world, but what stood out for Tim was Alex's advice about remembering and using people's names, because it can help build relationships. According to Tim, this advice has been extremely helpful in his role as a CPA Australia student ambassador on campus where he has had to build relationships with people that he is often meeting for the first time.

In his casual job at a retail business, Tim also started greeting regular customers by their name. As a result, he discovered he was building a genuine rapport with many people. Much to his surprise, one of those regular customers recently offered Tim a part-time accounting job at a multinational oil and gas company.

Tim is excited about the prospect of this new job, and says he can credit the opportunity entirely to asking the name of a stranger in an environment he had never considered would be meaningful to his career.

CHAPTER 14

TEAM WORK AND POOR TEAM PERFORMANCE

As an experienced CEO, I want you to know exactly how I view teams and the individuals within them. In your early years, you may well face rocky times, particularly in team settings. When you do, I want you to think about what the leader's perspective is—what they look for, how closely they observe and what you can do to be positively recognised for your efforts.

I always notice and nurture the team player who can set aside personal differences with a fellow team-member to deliver a quality performance. Leaders respond to team players who are focused on getting the job done. We want individuals who understand that group success can be much more powerful than individual success, because this tells us that they are selfless and understand the bigger picture. If they can avoid being weighed down by any team politics, not get distracted by gossip or rivalries, and continuously channel their energy into achieving the goal, I will reward that individual with more responsibility.

I do this because these are the behaviours and qualities of a future leader.

They are the people I respect and want to help progress, no matter what their rank or experience. If someone is the most junior in the team but I see and hear that they are contributing the most, and they are consistently a top performer, I have no issue giving them additional responsibility that may well exceed their rank. My reality is we have a goal, we need to achieve it, and I do not have time for employee protocols based on rank rather than performance. You perform, I reward. Performance really does speak louder than words. Keep focused on that fact, no matter how tough the circumstances might be, because it is the truth of business.

So what happens if you start in a new job and come to realise that your team is underperforming or possesses an unfavourable reputation? I am not going to sugar-coat it: this can be a particularly tough circumstance to inherit. So if you do find yourself in this position, take a deep breath knowing that you will learn a lot about people, teams and other workplace realities.

You are yet to hold the authority to make changes that could benefit the team. Focus on the things that you can control and remember that the team does not have to define you. Remember brand 'You'? These are the times where it can really shine. Complete the tasks assigned to you and focus on exceeding expectations. For example, you might complete a report before the allocated deadline, or stay late to help a team member finish something they need help with. It is these little things that, over time, will add up to not only benefit the team, but also your reputation as a great team player.

By exhibiting these behaviours consistently, you will earn the kind of respect that enables you to raise team issues with the leader. The leader will likely listen because they recognise that your focus is in the right place and you can be trusted.

Remember, these sorts of conversations can be delicate. If the leader is aware of the problem—like the team is not delivering on its targets, for instance—he or she will be under pressure. People react to pressure differently so this is something you should try to identify in your leader early on in order to establish how you should raise the problem (remember the respectful curiosity I mention in chapter 12?) Visualise how your leader will likely respond to the issues you want to raise: are they typically a defensive person? Are they open to feedback from employees at all levels? Do you have a rapport with the leader so they will feel comfortable talking to you about what might be a sensitive matter?

Be very careful with your wording and always be constructive. Also, ensure you have done everything within your power to attempt to remedy the issue and provide examples of this. Articulate why you believe the issue is preventing the team from functioning more effectively or harmoniously, and then offer a suggested solution. All of this will take some thought before you enter the conversation. Preparation is essential. Be solution focused.

Keep in mind that, despite the strong efforts you may make in your work environment, there is always a chance that they will go unrecognised. You can do something about that. When this happened to me, I recognised and recorded my key achievements on each occasion that I thought it was warranted. This proved extremely beneficial for me when I was seeking my next employment opportunity. I possessed a summary of my verifiable achievements that I could comfortably promote to my next employer. I did not and I do not wait for others to affirm my achievements because, while it is nice if they do, what matters more is that we know within ourselves what we earned.

To this day I am always looking to contribute positive outcomes into my black box.

MAKE IT HAPPEN: TURN AROUND A POORLY PERFORMING TEAM

Teamwork can be great. You often can achieve much more when you have the support and encouragement of a good group of people. However, you may find yourself in a team that is ineffective or dysfunctional. This situation is what I want to focus on with you and I want to be with you at those times because they are challenging, but formative.

Here is how you can help get a team back on track.

Ask questions

Instead of being frustrated about the lack of productivity and collaboration in your team, adopt a considered inquisitiveness into why it is happening. Wherever possible, have open and constructive conversations with your team members, because gaining their perspective may help you identify what lies at the core of the issue.

Influence morale

You may not be experienced enough to completely change the morale of the team, but you can try to channel the focus to what the team does well. Life has only two languages—positive and negative. Always be the person who speaks positively and you will find, sooner than later, that it will have an influence on a better team environment.

Always reinforce the collective sense of purpose because your leader will appreciate it.

Listen and act

A dysfunctional team can often be the result of people not listening to each other. The most important thing you can do in life and work is to exhibit respect for others—and at the core of that is the capacity to listen. If you are an attentive listener, people will increasingly be willing to share their perspectives with you. You will learn more about each and every person—from what motivates them to what worries them. When issues arise in the team, you may well be the person who provides a workable solution because of your holistic knowledge and deeper understanding of your colleagues.

Quotable quote from Alex

Leaders respond to team players who are focused on getting the job done. We want individuals who understand that group success can be much more powerful than individual success, because this tells us that they are selfless and understand the bigger picture.

Be sensitive to diversity

If you see a team member who is being alienated or disrespected, explicitly or passively, because of their beliefs or lifestyle choices, be the bigger person and ensure that they feel included. This can be as simple as making sure they are invited to various after-work activities.

Remember, you are on the leadership journey and that, ultimately, is about mobilising people. This can only be achieved when you are aware of and sensitive to who is in your team and how best to engage them on the journey.

Access educational support

If you notice within the team the issue is more about gaps in knowledge and capability, rather than effort, this might be something you can help address.

Given you likely left an educational environment recently, you will be attuned to programs that enhance management and business capabilities. Why not conduct some private research as to programs or courses that might be of assistance?

Raise your findings with your manager and suggest they might be worth a review. This type of behaviour demonstrates initiative, insight and a solution-focused manner that is always valuable in the workplace.

Socialise

I can't count the times that a dysfunction in the workplace came down to how little people really knew each other, in spite of working closely together five days a week.

I see enormous value in the social aspects that come from a workplace, but I am always conscious that the balance must be right. As a young professional it is a reasonable expectation that you will provide energy and a desire to interact that should add value in and of itself. Look to create opportunities for the team to communicate in social settings; sharing conversations over coffee, meals or celebrations, for instance, will enhance communication at the human level.

Take people momentarily out of the pressure cooker environment and observe the impact that has on their productivity—it's almost always positive.

DON'T FORGET

Here's what to take away on how to turn around a poorly performing team:

- avoid frustration with team members—talk to them and determine what lies at the core of the issue

- listen to people's concerns and respect their confidence

- don't let office politics and rivalries distract from your own performance

- remember that your positive work ethic and attitude will help influence team morale.

Get ahead of the pack

Here are some ways to really get your team working well together:

- *Do it:* Lead the way in finding common ground—and remember that food is often a great reflection of diversity. Each week, set a time for a team member to bring their favourite dish to work. Sharing a meal with a personal story behind it can help inspire a more relaxed dialogue. If you're having problems in a team environment, suggest you all go on a field trip or try something new. This could mean going for a coffee or trying a team-building exercise. Another option is a volunteer day together at a local charity. A change of scenery might help people gel more together.

- *Ask yourself:* After a disagreement or an issue with someone, ask yourself what was your contribution to it? Reflect slowly on this because that will bring out a more balanced truth.

Meet the mentee: Vivien Lei

Vivien Lei has two years left to complete her five-year combined Law and Commerce degree at the University of Auckland. Over this time, she will need to work in teams to complete a lot of group assignments, and she is wary of the challenges that come with making sure a team stays on track and everyone cooperates with each other.

Vivien struggled with the idea that the success of the team might be impacted by people not liking each other or having conflicting ideas. She sought some advice from Alex about how to manage those feelings so they wouldn't jeopardise the team's effectiveness.

Alex explained to her that the team members do not need to like each other, but they do need to work on developing a mutual respect for each other. Team members are much more effective and productive when they are showing respect for each other, so she should start listening to and observing people's positive qualities and utilising their strengths.

'I think it is difficult for people my age to comprehend that level of professional regard for team mates, but it makes sense that cooperating and carefully listening to other people's ideas is really important,' Vivien said.

Vivien now acknowledges that respecting your team mates can help to turn an unproductive team around. By showing respect and listening to those who do not think in the same way as you, or have the same perspectives or understandings on issues, you're able to take a multi-faceted approach to a challenge. Vivien mentioned that, during group work for her law assignments, taking this approach has helped her teams to deliver a more cohesive and well-rounded result for their projects.

'If you try to see things from other perspectives, you can come to a compromise and get the work done in a way that everyone is happy with,' she said. 'When there's a sign of conflict about the work, you have to realise that no-one's idea is wrong. You have to look at each point of view to spot any strengths and weaknesses so you can produce the best possible group effort.

'Alex's advice helped me to see that sometimes you have to take the time to really step back and listen to others. It can be hard but sometimes you have to consider other people's strengths to let someone else take the lead. Sometimes when it comes to leading a team you have to be humble and realise that you're not always the right person for the job.'

CHAPTER 15

GETTING PEOPLE TO SAY 'YES'

Throughout the journey of professional life, an ultimate aim is to have people say 'yes' to your ideas or instructions. It is key in standing out and being remembered. Early on in your career, however, you being the one saying 'yes' is more likely than you being the one hearing it. That is okay; you have still got a lot of learning to do and the expectation is for you to willingly undertake what is requested of you.

Having people agree with you comes down to your influencing skills. This will likely develop with experience but, even as you climb the ranks, it will remain a day-to-day challenge. As a CEO, whether it is a tough negotiation, encouraging a staff member to take on an extra task, or seeking the board's approval for an idea that will take the business into uncharted territory, influencing a desired answer remains an ongoing leadership challenge. It is also an art that some people find easier than others: some people possess an inherent ability to sway opinion, whereas others struggle.

If you fall within the latter category, what you should start focusing on early in your career is building the foundation for people to want to agree with your ideas. My experience is that, along your professional journey, if you encourage people to say 'yes' to a much smaller challenge, and prove it was the right path, they are more likely to agree to the next challenge. This will build a trust momentum and your reputation for successfully following through on a new idea.

Some of the big 'yes' requests I ask for today as a CEO I would not have asked for five years ago when I commenced the role. But, along with my team, we have earned our stripes. We can now evidence current performance and past achievements as part of the reason the board should feel confident about new initiatives.

Remember, timing is imperative. Picking the right time of day or week to raise your idea or suggestion will help ensure it gets the best hearing. If the authority figure is distracted by other issues, you'll likely receive an undesirable answer. Ensure you speak to them at a time where you have their undivided attention.

You also have to be able to position your idea in a simple story-telling mode. Remember how you would sit on the mat in the classroom at primary school, listening to the teacher read a story? Think about how mesmerised you were and how you wanted to hear more. You have got to become a storyteller and capture people with a great opening, a succinct middle and a captivating end.

Test yourself that you do believe your idea is a worthy way forward and that you're confident it will result in a successful outcome. If you don't believe in it, don't ask for the opportunity. Be honest about any perceived risks and be open about the path you're going to take to reach the objective. This might surprise you, but don't be afraid to be 'human', because it may well break the tension of whatever it is you're trying to get across the line.

One single example of allowing yourself to be 'human' from my experience was when I was negotiating a deal with another business. I went into the meeting with a mandate not to spend any more than a certain amount of money and, naturally, the person I was sitting across the table from possessed a mutual determination, although with a different figure. Both of us were at significant risk due to our senior roles and what was at stake for both organisations. After a long conversation, we got to a point where we just could not agree on the dollars. We were like two bulls in the pen—neither of us would budge.

Then, completely on impulse, I placed the keys to my personal car on the table and said, 'I am not going to pay you the amount you want, but I will give you my car. I have owned it for a long time and it means a lot to me. I have come to like you and I recognise your situation, so I want you to have it—it is a gesture and a sign of respect. You can add the value of the car to my numerical offer, but there is no way I am going to have my business pay you anything over this. I know you are in a corner, you know I am in a corner, so take my car on top of the money I have offered and let's call it a deal.'

This may sound extreme, but my action brought the conversation back to a much more human level. The man across the table said he would not take the car, but he now understood that I was not going to budge on my monetary offer, and we signed the deal.

What you can learn from this is that people will likely say 'yes' when they believe you are who you appear to be, that you are authentic. Once they make that judgement, and they must make that in their own time, they will feel safe in the decision they make, even if it is an uncomfortable one. That man and I developed a mutual respect: he recognised my gesture was genuine and the human connection allowed us to close a commercial deal.

MAKE IT HAPPEN: GETTING OTHER PEOPLE TO SAY 'YES'

To be influential and to develop leadership skills, you need to give in order to gain the respect of your colleagues. During your career you may want other people to endorse your ideas, or approve particular projects or pieces of work. Sometimes this will happen easily, while other times you may encounter resistance. So how can you influence people to back you?

Respect your audience

During your career you will be asking a variety of people at different levels of seniority to say 'yes'. Be very focused on the importance of respect and protocol. It remains my view that if you're presenting to a person or a group well above your station, you should refer to them as 'Mr' or 'Ms' and wait for them to tell you to call them by their first name. This immediately defines your ability to respect, which can only help your objective.

Know your audience

Before I attend any meetings internally or externally, I request a brief on the background of the people I am meeting, primarily because it enhances my ability to better engage with them. Almost always you will find common interests and that is a wonderful human way to make meetings more effective and relationships more interesting. This will lay a solid platform on which to receive the answer you're looking for.

Believe it

Believe in what you're telling people. They're not going to agree with you if your body language and tone of voice indicate you don't believe it yourself. Deliver your message with confidence.

Read the signs

Tune in to what other people say. Listen to the factors that they find important in a decision-making process and address those factors when presenting your idea or opinion to them. This way you will be able to proactively address many of their potential concerns and questions before they are even presented.

Quotable quote from Alex

People will likely say 'yes' when they believe you are who you appear to be, that you are authentic. Once they make that judgement, and they must make that in their own time, they will feel safe in the decision they make, even if it is an uncomfortable one.

Be a good communicator

Tell people your idea in a story with a concise beginning, middle and end. Observe whether people are engaged and be willing to vary your style if you see it's not working. Frame the question or statement in a positive way. Think precisely about what you're going to tell your colleagues and use constructive language when delivering your information. Remember, people always respond to a genuine attempt to provide solutions to a problem.

Do your homework

Make sure you have done your research, worked through all aspects of your idea and are prepared to answer any questions presented to you. Know your facts, and the pros and cons of what you're asking someone to say 'yes' to.

Provide evidence

Do you have examples of how your idea will positively affect your team's work? Has a similar idea been used elsewhere with a positive outcome? Use these instances as evidence to back up your idea and provide people with more reasons to agree with you.

Be patient

Influencing people can take time and energy. A change of direction requires resilience and a willingness to be there for the full journey. In many examples a new idea has taken years to ultimately be executed. Focus on what you can influence.

DON'T FORGET

Keep in mind the following when moving others to a 'yes':

- earning people's trust is key
- don't rush in—picking the right time to discuss your idea is imperative

- plan your communication in advance
- possess a thorough understanding of the person you're speaking with—what have they responded positively to in the past?

Get ahead of the pack

Here's how to really build on your convincing skills:

- *Do it:* Much of life is about negotiation, and practising your skills with those you know can really help. Pick an issue that someone in your family has a very strong view on. Take the opposite position to them and see how successful you are in building the case to change their mind. This will be a trial and error process—keep practising.

- *Ask yourself:* Have you identified the people you may have to influence? On what basis did you make that choice? Do you know enough about them? The answer to these and other questions will come from the increasingly good habit of getting to know the people around you.

Meet the mentee: Emma-Jaye Bernhardt

UTS Bachelor of Business student Emma-Jaye Bernhardt always dreamed of applying her business and accounting knowledge to a creative industry. But her current role with a global asset management company also comes with the challenge of having to convince people to agree with her ideas.

The Sydney student, who is currently balancing working with completing her marketing major, received some mentoring from Alex when she featured in an episode of The Naked CEO web series. He recommended that developing team-building skills should always be a priority and that the best way to build confidence is to earn others' trust. This would always put her in a good position to influence others and gain their cooperation.

'At the core of everything you do—it's all about building relationships with people,' Alex told her.

He encouraged her to believe in herself and reminded her that the best way to get a good response from your team members is to find a positive way to encourage and mobilise them into action.

Emma-Jaye said that Alex's encouragement and enthusiasm gave her a lot more confidence, especially when heading into her new role where she is often required to pitch ideas and concepts to a large team of people, most of whom are considerably older than her.

She has learnt that the best way to get people to say 'yes' to an idea is to trust yourself, be confident and to prepare by gathering all available information before asking someone to commit to your concept.

Communication, high standards in principles of team-work, and strong leadership skills are among the key qualities that Emma-Jaye says she has learnt to focus on since speaking with Alex. When looking for a positive response to any suggestions she makes, Emma-Jaye chooses her target audience wisely.

'Before asking somebody to do something for you, it's important to work out what their strengths are, because if you try to get them to agree to something they're not interested in or really don't want to do, it's not going to be done to a high standard, or maybe at all,' she said.

Emma-Jaye says she will continue sharing her ideas and opinions with her colleagues and managers, but that she will make sure that she also listens to other people's pitches and opinions because that mutual respect is one of the most important things she now values about working in a team.

PART IV
BE THE BEST
PERSON YOU CAN BE

Being all that you can be is not a static event. You must look to consistently push the limits of your abilities by working as hard as you can. Never lose the hunger to extend yourself. The more difficulties you face, the more you will surprise yourself about what you are capable of. I have a view that all people have more energy and capability in them than they think. You will never know what you are truly capable of if you do not consistently test yourself in new and perhaps difficult circumstances.

I really want to press that consistency message. In the workplace, others having certainty in you will build trust and respect. People want to be able to rely on you. The only surprise you want to present people with is your ability to exceed their expectations.

The workplace is an observant environment so you need to make every effort to do your best at everything you apply yourself to. Early on in your career, you might be asked to fulfil rather menial or seemingly thankless tasks but, trust me, people will be observing your attitude and response. Demonstrating your willingness and putting as much effort as you can into a variety of tasks will speak volumes for the sort of person you are. By consistently exhibiting a positive and willing attitude, you will build a strong and respected brand 'You'. Your energy is infectious, so make it the positive kind.

People can sense when someone is not applying everything they are capable of. Half-heartedness is a respect repellent. You are not going to get everything right, but if your manager and colleagues know you're trying your hardest, people will see the best in you. This comes down to consistently exhibiting a positive work ethic and attitude—and, more importantly, that you are willing to take on responsibility and instruction. Even if your best does not result in the desired outcome, people will be far less critical if they know you have made a genuine effort.

What if you feel like you're putting in your best effort, but it becomes evident that you're not meeting your manager or colleagues' expectations?

They might tell you that a certain task you have completed is not good enough. Or they may say nothing but you notice that they have amended what you have produced so it barely resembles what you submitted. Whatever the circumstances, understand that it is up to you find a solution. Pay attention to their feedback, adapt your approach and persist. If this proves ineffective and they still seem unhappy, approach them. Ask what you could be doing differently, what you could improve or might have an issue with. This will put the onus on them to explain why they seem unsatisfied with your work. Do not be afraid of asking, and do not be hurt by their feedback or criticism. Take it on board. Be open and willing to ask that question. Every bit of pain is a building block for your ever-growing character.

But what if things are going well and you are feeling confident in the role?

Ensure you do not make the mistake of resting on your laurels because it can breed a lingering complacency. Every few weeks, ask your manager if they require anything extra of you. If not, that is fine—but ensure you're always looking to embark on new experiences and develop new skills.

Feeling comfortable in a role is a double-edged sword. Sometimes you feel it because you are in a role that you enjoy, it is still stretching you and you are still learning things. That is my version of comfort. Where I am not okay with the term 'comfort' is when you are in a role you find easy—maybe the money is also good and you like the people you work with—but, as a result, you have stopped learning. For too many years I have seen very talented colleagues lock their lives into that state and live to regret it. Sure, pause for a while if things feel comfortable, and enjoy it, but if, after that pause, the role does not the pass the 'Am I growing?' test, it is time to leave.

Do not wallow in a comfort zone for too long.

There is nothing like putting your head on the pillow at night, knowing that you put in your best that day or overcame a significant challenge. It will instil you with a tremendous sense of self-fulfilment and purpose, and people will notice.

CHAPTER 16

GETTING ORGANISED AND GETTING THINGS DONE

Before too long, multiple stakeholders will begin to demand more of your attention and input. Believe me, this is positive—being needed is a great acknowledgement of your station in the business and represents the beginning of your accountability journey that will grow as you grow.

Your ability to prioritise and multi-task will increasingly be called upon. Prioritising comes down to an understanding of context: when you are new, you really have little perspective of what is more important than something else. It is okay to ask your manager, but they will quite rapidly expect you to be able to gauge what the priorities are.

Consider organisation the backbone of your professional efficiency. It requires close attention and consistent tinkering. This comes naturally to some; they are inherently organised in their approach to life so they transfer this nature into the workplace. For others, however—and I fell within this group when I was younger—it is something that needs to develop. If that sounds like you, I highly recommend you get on with it immediately.

I have witnessed many promising young people falter due to their disorganised approach. Either they would wait until the last minute to complete their tasks, frustrating their colleagues in the process, or they would unwittingly over commit themselves and miss important deadlines as a result. Another problem disorganisation cultivates is an inability to effectively communicate when actions will be implemented and completed and these are key expectations of all employees, no matter their rank.

Keep your organisational approach personal — everyone's process varies. Some people write a 'to-do' list every morning and tick off tasks as they go; whereas others, like me, arrange their priorities in their head. It is important to find the process that works for you and turn it into a habit. You're aiming to make it an intuitive process, a system that you can take anywhere with you in your career. For me, I must begin each day with a morning walk, no matter what time, because this more than anything allows me to order my priorities of a day. This is my personal process.

Organisation skills are not just about achieving the daily outcomes. As you grow on your leadership journey, planning ahead becomes essential. Identifying your priorities and fitting them into a framework spanning a period of time will help you streamline your activities, preventing any conflicts in terms of deliverables, and helping you feel more on top of things in the process.

It will not just benefit you. Your colleagues and stakeholders who rely on you will feel much more confident in your ability if they see you are an organised operator. People tend to respond much better to certainty and clarity. For instance, if you can confidently answer a colleague's questions about the progress of a particular project and when it will be completed, even if your answer is not entirely what they want to hear, they will respond to you more positively than if you were to tell them you're not sure.

As part of your development you will be increasingly responsible for meeting deadlines. If you aim to achieve every deadline that you commit to, your organisational skills must be sharp. Remember, at times in your career you will not meet a deadline due to a range of events, but it is your responsibility to ensure that one of those events is not your inefficient organisational skills.

If you aspire to become an effective leader, know this: you cannot organise other people until you have learnt to organise yourself.

MAKE IT HAPPEN: GETTING ORGANISED

Being disorganised, like most things, is a set of learnt behaviours. Usually people are this way as a result of having had everything done for them as a child, or from perhaps being told exactly how to do things. Maybe they are just inexperienced in multi-tasking.

If you have had the luxury of being disorganised, remember—you are entering the workforce and it is time to learn some new behaviours.

Build a routine

Create a daily routine and stick to it. Set times for checking emails, completing tasks, making calls, or whatever you need to get done. Be strict with your time and it will help you get used to meeting deadlines.

Create reminders

Particularly during busy times we all need to be reminded of upcoming commitments. Develop a system that works for you. Calendar and phone prompts work best for me.

Quotable quote from Alex

If you aspire to become an effective leader, know this: you cannot organise other people until you have learnt to organise yourself.

Expect the unexpected

Even though it is always good to create a daily routine and stick to it, being flexible when circumstances change is also important. As a CEO, I always greatly appreciate those colleagues who can be flexible when I need them to be.

Break down projects

Instead of looking at a project in its entirety, break it down into mini project phases. It will not feel so overwhelming that way. If you mentally reward yourself for completing each phase, the experience will likely become much more positive.

Eliminate distraction

The word distraction takes on many dimensions. Over the years I have seen people be distracted by their untidiness, their proximity to others, social media accounts and general lack of concentration. When you begin in a role, focus is king so observe and eliminate those things that distract you. It will have a powerful impact on your capacity to be efficient and on the perspective that leaders have of you.

DON'T FORGET

Keep in mind these main points when getting organised and getting things done:

- being disorganised places you and others under needless pressure
- organisation skills are a universal expectation in the workplace
- find the process that works best for you and stick to it
- always plan for tomorrow.

Get ahead of the pack

Take your organisation skills to the next level with the following:

- *Ask yourself:* Do you find yourself often being more reactive than proactive? Simply responding to the work environment around you might be acceptable early on, but it is not the habit you want to create. Look for opportunities to show initiative.

- *Do it:* As you gain more experience, you will begin to recognise issues before they arise. For example, you might be working in a team and be the only one to notice that someone's upcoming annual leave will likely cause disruption on a given project. Be proactive and use your initiative. Raise the matter with your manager and suggest a possible solution.

Meet the mentee: Rhiannon Kirby

Rhiannon Kirby is no stranger to the challenge of staying organised and getting things done. Since 2011, the Perth student has juggled three jobs with studying at Curtin University.

'I had no idea if I was doing the right thing and taking the right approach to getting experience, or if I was just overloading myself for no reason. I wanted to know if employers would look favourably upon my ability to keep organised and stick to a busy routine, or if they would see the way I divided my time as a negative,' Rhiannon said.

Rhiannon was looking for reassurance and feedback on whether to continue to maintain her busy calendar. The opportunity presented itself when she received an invitation to spend a day at CPA Australia head office to meet Alex and his management team.

During a one-on-one mentoring session, Alex reassured Rhiannon that the skills she was developing in time management, being organised and completing multiple tasks on a strict time line were invaluable. He told her that as well as gaining a wealth of valuable life experiences, she was gathering the skills necessary to get things done in a busy and successful career.

Rhiannon says that, following Alex's advice to stay organised and to persist with her multiple workloads, she trained herself to create and maintain a very structured timetable. Rhiannon embraced technology and used syncing to ensure that her timetable and to-do list were available to her on all of her devices. She believes that following this strict calendar method is the key to her successfully achieving everything that she needs to.

Rhiannon says that planning ahead plays a big part in staying organised and getting things done. 'If I have things to get done, like assignments, I make sure that I always stay on top of knowing when something is due so I can make time to get everything done.'

After meeting with Alex and talking about her routine and organisational habits, Rhiannon felt a renewed sense of confidence and energy for her busy life, and a sense of the value that her experiences would add to her employment prospects. She wanted to make sure that her busy lifestyle was contributing to a career achievement, so she set herself a short-term goal of obtaining a graduate position.

In 2014, Rhiannon's efforts paid off when she was offered casual work as an undergraduate at KPMG. She is optimistic this will grow into a graduate role once she completes her university studies in 2015.

CHAPTER 17

SPOTTING AN OPPORTUNITY AND STANDING OUT

Not every opportunity to stand out and impress is obvious. Your boss will not necessarily gift one to you and you certainly should not assume you are entitled to it. This is equally true when you are setting plans for future career opportunities.

Opportunities can be like diamonds in the rough that only hard work, an open mind and willingness to take on new experiences will help you uncover.

When at work, the key is not to appear limited by your job description or title. For instance, you may encounter a moment where a duty is delegated to you and your reaction will be, 'This is not part of my job.' Under the pressure of the day-to-day grind, and everything else you have on your plate, you may be reluctant to take on anything over and above your specified role. Resist this temptation. Know that an additional task could be the door to a trove of opportunity—such as building relationships with new people, contributing to a broader area of the business or expanding your skill set—so do not immediately turn your back on them. If you have the capacity and your direct manager gives you the all clear, accept the challenge and commit to it.

I will give you an example. As CEO, I sometimes delegate a particular responsibility to someone who, on paper, is not the most obvious choice. I usually do this because I have seen a quality I like in that particular individual and want to test them, to see if they will rise to the challenge. By doing this, I'm giving them an indirect compliment: I have been impressed by their consistent positive attitude and performance, and as a result I believe they are a hard worker and possess the eagerness and courage to step up to something bigger. I take great joy in observing how the particular individual fares, and, more often than not, they successfully step up—surprising themselves more than anyone else in the process.

Some people become all consumed by a fear of failure when they identify an opportunity to accomplish something special, either in their current role or in the risk of taking on a new job. They perceive the pressure to achieve is just too great and they succumb to an irrational negativity about the potential consequences if they're not successful, like a fear they will be embarrassed or disappoint people. Consequently, these people fool themselves into thinking the opportunity is not a risk worth taking, so turn their back on it. I cannot emphasise enough that you must not do this, particularly at the beginning of your career. It will breed a restricting, negative habit that will hold you back throughout your working life. Cast fear from your mind knowing that the negative consequences of consistently refusing opportunities is a far greater risk in itself. You will stunt your self-confidence, narrow dimensions in terms of your skill set and limit your ability to relate to new people and experiences. Leaders are carved from good and bad experiences; in fact, most of my carving is from the latter. So if you have an ambition to lead, throw yourself at opportunities and work through the fear and it will become a habit.

If you can maintain a childish positivity, curiosity and a borderless mindset, you will always be transported to better places. Grasp hold of opportunities and ride them for all they are worth. I assure you that people in senior positions will notice, and will appreciate your appetite and courage to go above and beyond the expected. This will set you apart in a glowing spotlight, irrespective of the result.

Find those diamonds in the rough.

MAKE IT HAPPEN: HOW TO SPOT OPPORTUNITIES AND STAND OUT

Many students have asked me how to best stand out and seize an opportunity, either in their current role or when searching for the next career challenge. It takes an ability to identify what that opportunity is, together with resilience and hard work to convert it. From the earliest time I can remember, I got into the habit of sniffing out opportunities; however, it took me much longer to get into the habit of hard work to convert them.

So whether in your current position or looking for the next role, the following sections provide some basics.

Be a public person

No matter your personality type, speaking with colleagues from all areas of the business is essential. Be interested in what they do and make time to better understand their environment. More often than not in an informal chat, emerging opportunities will become part of the dialogue.

Become the 'go to'

Early on, work to build trust and confidence such that people naturally come to you to bounce off ideas and share their issues. A genuine rapport will always open the door to different worlds that you might want to be a part of.

Take the time to analyse

The best question you can ever ask is 'why?' It is amazing how many opportunities you may discover if you give yourself some time to think about why things are the way they are. Try to come up with possibilities of how they could be improved. If you have an inquisitive nature, hold on to that and follow your intuition.

Do not wait to be asked

As a CEO, I always remember colleagues who are willing to communicate their thoughts, ideas or initiatives without being asked. While they do not always receive the response they want, I put them in my positive memory bank as someone who is willing to have a go. Sooner or later, I find a way to match them to a new opportunity.

> ### *Quotable quote from Alex*
>
> Cast fear from your mind knowing that the negative consequences of consistently refusing opportunities is a far greater risk in itself. You will stunt your self-confidence, narrow dimensions in terms of your skill set and limit your ability to relate to new people and experiences.

Make the most of chance encounters

I remember once being told at the airport that my flight was delayed for eleven hours. As I walked away, I told the man approaching what he was about to hear. Long story short, by the time we got on the flight I had hired him. Remain interested in people and you never know what might happen.

Think outside the square

When looking for a new job, have a look at the approaches you are taking to make contact with employers. Does a potential avenue to engage the employer exist outside the standard online application? Perhaps a handwritten letter to the Human Resources Manager? As always, use your uniqueness to stand out.

DON'T FORGET

Remember these tips for spotting opportunities:

- be bigger than your job description
- always look out for opportunities and seize them
- step outside your comfort zone—it will speak well of your attitude
- build a reputation for being the 'go to' person.

Get ahead of the pack

Here's how to really get the most out of any opportunities you spot:

- *Do it*: From this day forth heighten your curiosity around everything you do. Start asking questions—not only about what goes on in your department, but also about what happens throughout the business. This will build your practical understanding and be a foundation for new ideas.

- *Ask yourself*: Identify similar businesses, both domestic and international, in your sector. How differently do they operate? What opportunities can you see by adopting some of their processes or marketing techniques? Prepare a two-page report outlining how other firms may be dealing with similar issues and highlight any opportunities for your own business.

Meet the mentee: Olivia Ross

Deakin University student Olivia Ross was one of many young people applying for graduate roles and, understandably, she had started to worry about how to stand out from the crowd and secure a job.

As many of her peers had focused their efforts on completing vacation roles to get work experience, Olivia feared that her decision not to take up vacation work would work against her.

Olivia had the opportunity to meet with Alex and shared her concerns about the recruitment process ahead. Alex told Olivia that the best way to stand out as a great graduate is to be herself, to show individuality and to prove that she is a young person with lots of initiative.

He told Olivia that to be noticed, she should enhance her opportunities to promote her personality by improving her communication and networking skills. This advice included handwriting letters to potential employers, learning more about people within the accounting profession that inspired her and trying different ways to network with them.

In response to Alex's advice Olivia started attending Toastmasters, a worldwide organisation that groups people together in various locations to practise public speaking.

She says that speaking publicly on impromptu topics at Toastmasters has been a great learning opportunity for her and that she is getting better at thinking on her feet and answering questions spontaneously. As a result, Olivia's confidence in her presentation skills has grown.

'When I start work I'll probably be giving presentations or addressing senior partners or other people above me who have already developed these presentation skills,' said Olivia. 'There will be other grads but not all of them will have these skills that I'm working on, which will help me stand out. It will show that I can work at a higher calibre than others.'

Alex also advised Olivia to stop worrying about the opportunities her peers had taken on the path to graduate recruitment. She should instead focus on which roles she would most enjoy and would suit her career goals. Rather than thinking about how she could stand out from all accounting graduates, she was able to narrow her focus on how to stand out for the roles she was actually interested in.

'Alex showed me that I was thinking about it all wrong. Instead of trying to make myself the person I thought everyone was looking for, I realised I should just highlight who I really am', said Olivia.

Using her newly refined networking and communication skills and confidence in her individual worth to help her stand out, Olivia ended up with not one but two offers for graduate positions in 2015. She chose to accept a role with Nexia, an accounting firm in Melbourne.

CHAPTER 18

SUCKING IT UP

It is as confronting as it is disappointing if you come to realise that you do not like your job. You were so excited about it to begin with, but now it is a nightmare. Learning to get through this realisation is one of life's lessons.

I know this may seem impossible, but it need not be. Instil a state of mind that while you cannot control everything and everyone around you, you can control how you react to them. A lot of it comes down to training yourself to think differently, more positively, to suck it up and get on with what you have been employed to do. I am telling you, it is an amazing feeling when you clear this mental hurdle. I only wish I'd worked it out earlier in my career!

If I could rewrite one thing in my early working life, it would be the near fatal mistake I made of assuming that, every time I did not like a job, the smartest thing to do was to quit and move on to something else. For about a decade I kept swapping roles in the belief that the flawless job was calling me. Of course, I didn't know what the flawless job looked like, but I was desperate to find it. A mission to nowhere, you might say.

Particularly in the early years of our career, we can suffer from an expectation gap that we create for ourselves. To protect yourself in those first jobs, lower your expectations of feeling completely fulfilled, or that everybody around you will be perfect. Just focus on the art of living with people. Get the basic job requirements done and familiarise yourself with the foreign concept of the working week.

I really struggled with those early years of transitioning to work. In reality, I was ill disciplined and far too immature to deal with the confronting and uncaring work environments that I walked into. On reflection, I realised it was not that they were uncaring; it was more that I was expecting the world to come to me, rather than I become part of the world. You have to play ball when you move into a new game. It took me too long to work that out. Do not make my mistake. Had I built early discipline rather than job-hopped, I would have begun my big life earlier. It was not until I was 30 that I began the process of creating my own universe, which had to be built on some very strong, disciplined experiences.

So what do I mean by 'sucking it up'?

It is finding the resolve to stay in a role you do not necessarily like until you learn how to like it and respect the people you do not want to be with. That is the discipline I kept avoiding in the false belief that I would find the one job out there that was perfect on all fronts.

In a job, your dislike might arise from the tasks asked of you, or the people you deal with, but never let these circumstances alone push you towards the exit door. If you stay and work through these issues, people will notice and greater responsibilities will come your way because of the maturity you are exhibiting. Often your views of the workplace will then change.

The more responsibilities you take on, the more people rely on you, so if you're keen to become a quality leader, you must suck it up and push through the tough times. Do not make a hasty decision to rush into a new job like I did; rather, understand and accept that your job will always have aspects you do not like, particularly at the early stage of your career.

So employ the attitude that you want to learn and you accept that might mean having to work through difficult relationships and complex circumstances, and undertaking tasks that you might not like. This will escalate your potential tenfold.

MAKE IT HAPPEN: HOW TO SUCK IT UP

The following provides some tips on how to look at situations and people in a new way when you're starting to feel your job might not be right for you.

Understand you

Resistance to certain tasks usually comes down to your personality. We all like to focus on the things we're good at, but the character-building experiences come from being gracious about the things we don't like doing. Reset your mind—you're no longer a student. You're beginning the journey of leadership. The sooner you learn to take instructions and act on them, no matter their nature, the quicker you will be the one issuing the instructions.

If only I had learnt that sooner!

Be decisive

Immediately begin the process of training yourself to be decisive and effective. No-one supports a procrastinator and no-one is going to do the work for you. Prepare well, complete tasks earlier when possible and aim to be decisive, particularly when others cannot or will not be. It may cause you some pain initially but it is better to be known as decisive rather than indecisive.

Quotable quote from Alex

We all like to focus on the things we're good at, but the character-building experiences come from being gracious about the things we don't like doing.

Pick the person challenge

As a positive exercise, make a point of challenging yourself to build an engagement with a person or group who clearly is not responding well to you. You will learn many things on this adventure. All of these learnings will come flooding back in the years to come when you are first charged with managing people. In many ways, building a relationship with someone you initially don't get along with is the most important exercise in your first couple of roles.

Put on your poker face

While I unabashedly remind you to be yourself, try not to wear your heart on your sleeve. I recall as a young man once 'losing it' in the workplace over the way I was being treated. I stormed into the manager's office shaking with rage and my boss simply said, 'Go for a walk. Come back when you've calmed down'. The longer I walked, the more embarrassed I became—to the extent that I nearly walked home.

The lesson was profound. I had to pluck up the courage to face up and apologise for my behaviour.

That day, I learnt I could never play competitive poker. No matter how enraged, frustrated or embarrassed you feel in the heat of the moment, just suck it up. Avoid expressing your negative emotions verbally or physically and remain professional at all times. You will spare yourself the need for an apology. When things calm down, take time to reflect either with a colleague or with a loved one.

Let learning be your friend

It used to drive me crazy listening to well-meaning adults telling me that life was about continuous learning. Now that I am a well-meaning adult, I agree with them. Your best friend at the worst of times in life—whether at work, at home or at play—is the principle of continuous learning. The tougher the times, the greater the potential for growth so celebrate those times rather than contest them.

DON'T FORGET

Here are some tips for overcoming negative feelings about a job or task:

- persevering during tough times builds character
- you can't always control your environment or other people's behaviour, but you can control how you respond to them

- strengthening your resilience will instil a positive and effective attitude

- don't be overcome by negative emotions—remain professional and remember you will always learn during difficult times.

Get ahead of the pack

Suck it up with the best of them with these tips:

- *Do it:* This might be difficult, but in the interest of building your character, volunteer to undertake a particular task at work that no-one else wants to do. Your colleagues will probably have mixed reactions, but your manager will likely have a positive perspective. This is a good place to start on the 'suck it up' journey.

- *Ask yourself:* Why don't you enjoy a certain task in your job description? Is it the boredom or the fear of failure that drives your emotion? Neither is helpful to your personal growth—when in doubt, 'suck it up'.

Meet the mentee: Alan Liang

Alan Liang had been struggling to balance the workload between his commerce degree at the University of New South Wales and a full-time job. Something had to give, and Alan was about to drop his tertiary studies and focus solely on his job. He had reached a point where he simply did not want to study any more. After all, many of his work colleagues held good positions without university qualifications.

It was around this time that Alan came across the 'Ask Alex' section of The Naked CEO, which over a series of events ultimately led him to a face-to-face meeting with Alex.

Alex gave Alan a lot of advice that day, but his main recommendation was that Alan should stick with his course and see the degree through to completion. 'Alex told me that since I had started the course I should keep going and finish what I'd started,' said Alan. 'He said that I should hang in there and complete the second half of my degree.'

Alex reminded Alan that throughout life, and particularly in his career, he would always have tasks that he would not want to do. The only way to progress and be successful in life would be to push through and get things done — even if he did not particularly enjoy it at the time.

He also reminded Alan that the experience of completing the course while working full-time would be character building. It would teach him discipline, time-management and self-belief. Despite it being a difficult and challenging task, Alex was sure that Alan would feel an enormous sense of accomplishment after graduating.

Alan realised the value of receiving advice from a business leader of Alex's rank and, after some consideration, he decided to follow Alex's advice rather than that of his colleagues. He says that it is one of the best things he has ever done. 'It was tough. I was working Monday to Friday and spending my entire weekends focusing on study and assignments. But I pushed through, and now I'm close to the end of my final semester,' said Alan.

Although the challenge of completing his degree has been a difficult one, and he has not enjoyed every single moment of the process, Alan says that he feels as though the experience has made him a better person and he is proud of everything he has achieved.

He is excited to graduate this year and is thankful for Alex's advice. He can see clearly now that having a university qualification will help to open more career doors and allow him to achieve greater long-term success.

CHAPTER 19

PUSHING BACK AND SAYING 'NO'

One of the dangers of being a young and enthusiastic employee is that certain colleagues might take advantage of your eagerness to please with excessive requests for your time and input. Suddenly your diary and 'to-do' list become inundated with pressing deadlines and meetings with various people from multiple areas of the business. If this happens, you may find yourself sinking under the weight of expectation and pressure to complete tasks over and above what your direct manager would have already assigned you.

The worst thing you can do is overcommit and not deliver, so avoid setting false expectations at all costs. While helping out where you can and being a proactive and cooperative team player is important, inevitably there will come a time where you will have to say 'no'.

FITTING YOUR RESPONSE TO THE CONTEXT

Pushing back on a colleague's request without coming across as unhelpful or difficult is tricky, so I will break it down into three common scenarios that should help you out.

The request comes from someone at your own level, or just above it

Saying 'no' is not a desirable response for you or the receiver. Therefore, you need to ensure you provide a good reason for why you're unable to perform a particular task.

If a colleague is applying pressure on you to be involved in a particular project but you're too busy to manage extra responsibility, communicate this to them with firm politeness. This is where your organisation skills (see chapter 16) will come in handy: you need to have a clear idea of what your priorities are and when they are due. If these are unrelated to what the colleague is asking, politely inform them of what you are currently working on, its significance to the business and the authority figure who is expecting to receive it. If you are caught on the hop, saying you will get back to them once you have checked your diary or spoken to your direct manager is okay, just ensure you do.

People will react differently to these responses. They might get offended or make you feel guilty, but stay strong and work through it because this test is one you need to learn how to master. The higher up the career ladder you climb, the more responsibility and demands you will face. Try not to be disheartened by any unfavourable reactions and build strength from the situation.

You want them to understand that you are saying no at that point in time not because you want to, but because you have to.

The request comes from someone senior

This is very different to the preceding scenario. When someone senior, who is not your boss, asks for your assistance, regardless of your existing responsibilities and deadlines, listen carefully to the request and understand you may well have to complete the task. At that point, however, you need to inform your direct supervisor of this request so they are aware that one of your other priority activities may be delayed. If your direct manager has any issues with the request it is up to him or her to deal with it, not you.

What if your boss sends multiple tasks your way, and you are confused about how to manage everything? Rather than accepting that and not delivering, or saying you cannot do it, organise a time to sit with them one-on-one to go through your list of priorities. Again, they will likely help you reshuffle your schedule and provide additional people to help if need be. If they do not, know that you raised the issue with them and just do the best you can to deliver—you might surprise yourself by what you are capable of. If you produce something that your manager finds less than satisfactory, at least you forewarned them about your predicament.

You have been asked to fulfil a task you do not agree with

The right of refusal is earned. What I mean by this is that the more experience you garner, the more you build your reputation as a valuable team player, inevitably, the more likely your colleagues will respect and adhere to your judgement. When you are a new recruit, however, understand it will be difficult to ascertain if a course of action you are asked to implement is ill informed.

In this circumstance, if you do have cause to believe there is an issue, gently offer up constructive alternative suggestions and options. Never lose sight, however, that your manager has employed you to follow direction.

Let me end with this. The one time you can undoubtedly say 'no' to someone is if what they are asking raises concerns about legalities or ethics. In a situation like that, do seek independent advice, but if refusing costs you your job, then so be it. Your welfare and personal brand are much too important to be jeopardised.

MAKE IT HAPPEN: HOW TO SAY 'NO' AT WORK

Saying 'no' is not something we are taught how to do when we are at university, nor is it something that comes naturally to most people in the first few years in the workplace. Naturally, we all want to please people, so quite often we will say 'yes' to things we perhaps should be saying 'no' to. The following section provides some help.

Understand why it's so hard

Normally no-one wants to come across as rude, disagreeable or unhelpful. You may not want to upset or anger the person asking, so you say 'yes' to keep the peace—but this can become a bad habit.

Professionally, you need to ask this of yourself: which is worse, the consequences of answering 'yes', which may bring an added workload that you're not in a position to handle, or the consequences of answering 'no', and perhaps upsetting someone? The more experience you get, the more obvious the answer.

Work on your reputation

You need to prove to those around you that you have a fantastic work ethic before you can be comfortable saying 'no'. Early on, you are in a great position to prove how eager and hard-working you are by saying 'yes' to as much as you can handle, and maybe even then some. Ironically, the more often you say 'yes' the more, in time, you will be able to say 'no'.

Work out what they really want

Don't just say you're too busy. Instead, ask questions to make sure you understand exactly what is required to complete the task. If you need to, ask for some time to think it over. Nothing is wrong with telling someone you will respond once you've had an opportunity to review the situation.

Quotable quote from Alex

The worst thing you can do is overcommit and not deliver, so avoid setting false expectations at all costs. While helping out where you can and being a proactive and cooperative team player is important, inevitably there will come a time where you will have to say 'no'.

Offer an alternative

When you're unable to take on a task, try to come up with another way to solve the person's problem. If the project is just too big for you to commit to in its entirety, maybe you could offer to help out on a smaller aspect of it.

Remember your team is there for a reason

If you're lucky enough to work with a group of people, or even another colleague, always consider the thought that perhaps they might appreciate the opportunity to work on the task, with or without you. Check with them first, get back to the requester and suggest you may have an alternate person.

Communicate

In all aspects of your life, including the moments of having to say 'no', clarity in communication is essential. People need to understand the reason for your decision. If you have been clear about the context, shown willingness to generally be collaborative, and indicated that you gave due consideration to their request, you have met a reasonable standard.

Don't confront

No matter how frustrated you might be with someone's requests, always remain calm. Process your words before you say them and, when you deliver your answer, make sure you avoid raising your voice or rolling your eyes. Body language is the truth the person sees.

Tell them eye to eye

In today's world we often see 'cop-out' communication delivered by email or text. Avoid that at all costs. Look someone in the eye and say 'no' with respect and confidence. When you're speaking with someone face to face, you can express your genuine interest in helping them out in some other way or at some other time. The effort that you have gone to in seeking them out sends a strong professional message. It's a good idea to follow up with a quick email to the requestor, outlining the main points of the discussion so there is a written record. This will help reduce any chance of confusion later down the track.

DON'T FORGET

Here are some tips for saying 'no' while still maintaining the respect of your colleagues:

- be willing to say 'no' when your existing commitments will be materially compromised

- be solution focused—if you don't have the capacity to perform the request, perhaps you can offer an alternative

- over-committing and setting false expectations is worse than pushing back on an additional request

- where possible, always seek to decline a request in person because this is more respectful—a follow-up email outlining the main points of the conversation is also sensible.

Get ahead of the pack

Say 'no' with integrity and confidence with the following:

- *Do it:* Proactively become involved in conversations about workplace topics and issues. During the dialogue, where relevant, bring in a contrary view and observe people's reactions, whether they be supportive or defensive. If you're going to say 'no' one of these days, you need to be able to engage in a full conversation to support your case.

- *Ask yourself:* What are you really afraid of? Think about what you fear the most about saying 'no' and why. Is this fear rational or not? Sometimes we do not spend enough time isolating the reasons we feel the way we do. Being able to articulate the reason will likely assist you in the approach you will take to say 'no'.

Meet the mentee: Rimal Prasad

If anyone can appreciate the difficulty of hearing the word 'no', it is Rimal Prasad.

The University of Auckland student suffered the self-confidence blow of twelve job application rejections in a row. This was tough at the time but, ultimately, created a great learning curve in empathy on his path to securing his dream role and teaching him the importance of saying 'no' graciously himself in the future.

But before he finally landed a job, Rimal was finding his self-confidence ebbing away under the constant feeling of rejection. During that time, he logged on to The Naked CEO website to ask Alex for advice.

Alex emphasised that everyone experiences failure or rejection at some point in their life. 'The fact is, the greatest lessons in my life have been through learning about my own internal strength when facing rejection—when being rejected for a job, or when facing difficult times in the work place or in life,' Alex said.

He encouraged Rimal to persist with his attempts to find a great job and to simply carry on with his career journey, using each rejection as an opportunity to learn what he could do better the next time. With this in mind, Rimal started to ask for feedback from employers who had rejected him and soon learnt that knowing of any weaknesses in his application and how he could improve on them helped him to build confidence and to keep trying.

He secured a part-time job as a loan assessor—a role where he was able to practise what he had learnt from having employers repeatedly say 'no' to him, when he himself declined loan applicants.

'I'm getting used to it now, but when I first started my job I was scared to say 'no' to people because I felt nervous anticipating their emotions and how they might react. But now I realise that it's part of every job, it happens all the time and you just have to be up-front about it,' Rimal said.

When giving someone bad news or turning someone down in a particular situation, Rimal has learnt that it is best to be direct and straight-to-the-point. He adds that it is important to give an honest explanation for why you are saying 'no', so that the recipient of the rejection isn't left guessing about your reasons for turning them down.

'What I will do is say, "Unfortunately, you were unsuccessful. But here's a good thing that you did. And here are the things you could do better and, if you work on them, I'm sure that next time you make an application you'll be successful",' said Rimal.

Rimal says Alex's advice helps him to communicate with empathy when he is delivering bad news. He knows how important it is to be transparent, kind and understanding when telling someone something they may not want to hear, especially when they may react poorly. He adds that Alex's advice about developing resilience is important for people on both sides of a 'no'.

'You need resilience to be on the receiving end of a refusal, but also to receive other people's feedback and reactions when you're saying 'no' to them,' said Rimal.

Rimal hopes that during his career he will be able to teach others both how to say 'no' but also how to deal with rejection. He will also try to show them that being rejected is not always a bad thing.

Ultimately, Rimal's journey after receiving Alex's advice led him to delivering the most important 'no' of his life so far. In 2014, Rimal was finally offered a graduate role at two Big 4 accounting firms. He says that it was hard to turn one down.

'Resilience taught me to get more experience, to really find myself and what I wanted from my career. Ultimately, my new experiences helped me decide where I wanted to work and where I could truly develop and be myself.'

Rimal used his new techniques to politely decline one of the offers and is thrilled to have secured the position of his dreams at PwC. He says that Alex's advice helped him to endure the hard road to success and to learn a lot along the way.

CHAPTER 20

WORKING OUT WHEN TO LEAVE

How do you know when it is the right time to leave a job? This is a question many young professionals ask me.

My advice is always the same: leave when you no longer feel like you are learning, developing professionally and nothing in the role is presenting you with new experiences. In my view, these reasons certainly lie at the core of the decision and they are your primary push factors. If you're considering handing in your notice because you don't like elements of the job, such as a particular task or colleague, these are unacceptable push factors. Remember what I wrote about sucking it up in chapter 18?

Leave when you are on top of the job. When you have built workable relationships that you thought were impossible to achieve with certain people. And when you have built at least a base level fondness for the role. That is really important.

Certainly today people are expected to have multiple job experiences, particularly compared to my generation. It is now more commonplace for young people to move roles after just a year or two, if not less. However, as a CEO—and I'm sure I'm not alone with this feeling—if I see a résumé of someone who has had three jobs in three years, it's still a major turn-off. It spotlights a person's inability to build a permanency and set up long-term relationships. This person, to me, has not sucked it up. I need to see evidence when I hire people that they have shown grittiness and an ability to stay in one place for a period of time, at least a minimum of two to three years.

WORKING OUT WHEN A PULL FACTOR IS ACTUALLY A PUSH FACTOR

Let me flip the coin: here are three push factors you may mistake as pull factors.

You feel safe

Being happy in a job is great, but you should not stay in it because you feel safe. I contend that seeking a position outside of your comfort zone is a far safer place, with much more personal satisfaction attached to it.

You're earning good money

Earning a salary or wage is always a great feeling, particularly when you first enter the workforce. I accept that in some circumstances you may have no choice for a period of time but to stay in a role—because you need to pay the rent, for instance.

However, I will agree to disagree with you if you told me that earning a lot of money is a worthwhile motivation to stay in a particular job. Money is an outcome; it should not be a motivation, particularly if you're young and are yet to have financial responsibilities such as a mortgage or dependants. Do what you love, and you will tend to do that well, leadership opportunities will open and the money will come.

You like the people you work with

Working with great people is wonderful, but what I have regularly found is that when someone stays in a job for solely that reason, they do not develop as much as perhaps they might have. A focus on your personal growth and ability to learn in a workplace should always come before your friendships with a boss or colleagues.

If you have made the decision to quit, know the reputation you leave behind in your job will be with your previous employer forever. You never know when you might work with someone again, who they might know, or when you might need them for a reference. At a personal level, ensure you leave for the right reasons; at a professional level, make sure your exit is well mannered and dignified.

MAKE IT HAPPEN: KNOWING WHEN TO LEAVE

If you are considering the decision to leave, weigh-up the advice provided in the following sections.

Identify what you do not like

Knowing what aspect you do not like about the job will help you define whether or not to leave it. Is it, for instance, the duties you do not enjoy, the culture of the organisation, or the value you derive from your position? Once you have identified the reason, or reasons, you will be in a much better position to weigh them up.

Ask whether you're still growing in the role

If you have identified the reasons you want to leave, balance them against questions like these: What are you learning in the role? What can you take to your next role? How will this experience make you a better person and employee?

Your answers to the questions should tell you whether leaving now or a little later is the better option.

Work out if just one negative issue is involved

Is this really about one negative situation that has got out of hand? If it is, absolutely do not leave until it is concluded satisfactorily or you have done everything humanly possible. It is always better to resolve any conflict in the workplace before you move on. If you don't learn the lesson from this, you may find that the same issue keeps presenting itself throughout your career.

Remember, it is important to own your own happiness and accept responsibility for some of the things you do not like. You are the only one who can make a change. You will note that I appear to have no interest in whether you are the perpetrator of this issue or not—it does not matter. Sort it.

Phone a family member or friend

In facing a difficult workplace issue, sometimes your friends and family will be able to offer a fresh perspective. You're also more likely to listen to and hear reason in their opinions because you trust them. They may be able to offer insights gained from similar experiences that could help you greatly.

Quotable quote from Alex

If you're considering handing in your notice because you don't like elements of the job, such as a particular task or colleague, these are unacceptable push factors.

Get some perspective

One of the great lessons I learnt from my parents whenever I felt down was that there is always someone worse off than you. As long as you have your health, you are rich. The important thing to remember, then, if you're facing difficult circumstances is to step back and understand it is just a job. It doesn't define you as a human being. So, don't let it get you down. Maintain your perspective.

Go the extra mile

I have to own up to something: I am a fierce competitor. In other words, I do not like to lose. For me, losing would be where I left a job in a bad set of circumstances. I lost a few times and learnt to dislike the taste.

So it should come as no surprise that I think that if you found yourself in a job you're really not enjoying, you should stick it out until you're positive about it. Leave then, a winner.

Think now about your next interview

This is not breaking news — your next employer will ask you why you left your last job. So now is the time to fix your current circumstances and relationships so you can answer that question with verifiable confidence. To put it in artistic terms, paint the picture that you will be able to frame and give to the next employer. And this picture has to be better than saying, 'I left because I didn't like it.'

DON'T FORGET

Here are some points to remember when working out whether the time is right to leave a position:

- identify what's driving your decision to leave and whether these aspects are really that bad — if not, suck it up

- speak to experienced people you trust about what you're considering and why — seeking counsel is a good idea if you're unsure

- job-hopping is a bad habit and doesn't reflect well on your résumé — making a kneejerk decision could be a regretful move

- the world is small and the reputation you leave behind will be with your previous employer forever — when leaving, make a dignified exit.

Get ahead of the pack

Take the time to really work out whether the time is right to leave a role with the following:

- *Do it:* Force yourself to write down alongside each other the reasons for staying and the reasons for leaving the job you're in. Weigh them up against each other and look for an obvious imbalance. This will likely help you work out whether a reason to leave really is as significant as you think it is.

- *Ask yourself:* What are the areas of personal growth that you need to consider? Have these opportunities for growth been exhausted in this role? Your most honest personal insights matter a great deal here. Growth opportunities should override all other reasons in your career and life.

Meet the mentee: Alistair Green

While studying a Bachelor of Pharmacy at the University of Queensland, Alistair Green took on a part-time job as a signage distributor. With no set work hours and a purely autonomous workload, he soon discovered that he did not enjoy the work. After a few months he wanted to quit.

After meeting Alex on campus and receiving a video message from him via The Naked CEO website, Alistair was inspired to think a little differently about the value that he gained from the job opportunity.

Alex encouraged Alistair to learn from any job, even if it was not his dream role or something long term. Alex also emphasised that he should only leave a job when he had learnt to love it.

'Perseverance is the key thing,' Alistair said. 'I did have disdain for the job and didn't feel that it was right for me and wanted to jump ship. But now, I look back at the role a bit differently.

'To begin with, the independence involved with the job was a little bit unnerving and I felt as though there was no support,' Alistair said. 'But what I found was that, in the end, the independence helped me to grow as a person—it taught me a lot about responsibility.'

Working alone and setting his own routine allowed Alistair to develop time-management skills as well as flexibility and autonomy. He proudly states that although the part-time work did not seem like an integral part of his career development, he did actually learn to love the job and ended up staying in the role for more than two years.

Today Alistair does not look at the short-term value of a job, but at the benefits that each experience will bring over the long term. How a role can help both prepare him for the future and identify his career goals is now his focus.

After persevering with the signage distribution role, Alistair moved to New South Wales to commence a Bachelor of Commerce at the University of Sydney. The time-management skills he learnt while distributing posters are already putting him in good stead as he balances his university course load with a newly obtained cadetship at Deloitte. He says that the lessons he learnt from Alex can be applied to almost any situation throughout a career.

Alistair acknowledges that in every job there will be some aspect that he does not enjoy, but that each element of a role will challenge him and give him opportunities to grow. Plus, there is always an opportunity to improve a situation.

Alistair says that he now focuses on where a future role will take him rather than whether or not he will enjoy it. He also intends to speak honestly with his employer about any aspect of a role he doesn't enjoy, and maybe they will work with him to come up with ways to change the situation.

PART V
THE LEADERSHIP TRACK

Every day you are at work is another important step along the leadership track. Even the experiences that may at the time seem completely insignificant will undoubtedly play a part in shaping you as a leader. So what is most important during this journey is ensuring that you are guiding yourself with the most beneficial intent and focus.

I believe that most people on the leadership track fall within two categories: those who have always wanted to become a leader, and those who have not given it much thought.

Early in my life I fell within the first category: my overarching career objective was to 'become the boss'. I did not know what I wanted to be the boss of, but my youthful imaginings of what such a role would entail—authority, salary and a big desk—projected a worthwhile station to strive towards. To me, being the boss equalled success.

Yet, as I progressed to the end of my schooling, I came to realise that I actually wanted to become a teacher. Even when I was suspended from school, teaching was the only profession that genuinely interested me. Working with students seemed like a fulfilling and challenging life, something I was certain I would be good at. This certainty came from my instinct, which kept telling me the same thing.

The problem was, however, this goal did not seem conducive to my long-held ambition of what 'success' looked like. I was 'born to rule', after all. Consequently, I ignored my passion to teach. Regrettably, this blind ambition led me down a long and hazardous track.

During the first ten years of my career, I was so distracted by my desire to reach the peak of the ladder I forgot to focus on each rung. These rungs—experiences, challenges, mistakes, all the lessons I've written about in previous chapters—are in fact what shape a leader. Not being focused on making the most of these not only limited my progress, but, even more critically, also blinded me to the fact that I was working in an area I harboured little passion for. I was oblivious—my tunnel focus on becoming the boss had rendered me closed-minded, which is simply the worst mindset for anyone at any stage of their life.

So, after a decade of applying this misguided focus and not reaching the heights I had envisioned, I finally had a moment of awakening: I would never attain a leadership position without following my heart. No-one would promote someone whose heart was not in it—which mine clearly had not been. It saddens me when I see highly talented individuals of any age whose body language tells me their heart is not in what they do.

My awakening was not easy to come to terms with. Admitting to myself that I had made the wrong choice all those years ago was an incredibly difficult reality to accept. I now know that I should have celebrated this insight, as you should do if it happens in your life.

Teaching still sparked a genuine curiosity in me. It filled me with a confidence that I could do it, and do it well. I wanted to work with young minds and felt like I had something to offer. So, I finally found the courage to pursue it, entering my first teaching job with a very different motivation to what had previously guided me. I was not there to become the boss. I was there because I sincerely wanted to be. I loved coming to work each day. A direct result of my passion for the role was the teaching accolades and leadership positions I would later garner. These were fantastic by-products of my passion for the job.

Today, it seems ludicrous that I didn't go straight into teaching. I am just glad that I eventually did because it proved the best career decision I ever made.

Ensure your motivation is not misdirected like mine was. Your focus should be on working in a role you are passionate about, not pursuing a leadership role for leadership's sake. This sort of focus is a limiting mindset. Those who avoid clouding their vision with an over-focus on 'destination leadership' are more likely to find it much quicker.

If you don't have an obvious passion to pursue, that is okay, and pretty common. Focus on gaining good practical experience but begin with the habit of searching for what you would really love to do. If you try hard enough, it will come. Talk to people, read articles and the newspapers, watch movies, follow politics, open your mind to the possibilities. To this day I keep doing that. Along with my morning walks, it is my most valued personal habit.

So what do I mean by genuine passion?

It is not something you say you have on your résumé because you think you should. What I know is that passion is a deep, primal emotion that's obvious to those around you. It is a connection that instils you with superhuman energy. You wake up each morning ready and looking forward to the day ahead. You care about what you do and you believe in it. Sound like a fantasy? I have every confidence your passion is out there for you to find, and you just have to believe it, fight for it and persist in your search if you have to. Nothing great comes easily, unless you are unlucky enough for it to happen so.

If you feel you know where your passions lie, have the insight and courage to align them with your career, or pursue them outright. If you get on that track, I believe your ascent to leadership will progress organically because it will be in a career you love.

Remember, leadership is about mobilising others to a greater cause. Do as I do is far more compelling than do as I say. An inherent passion is the greatest mobiliser of all.

Part V is designed to articulate the mindset you will need when you reach your leadership roles. Now is the time to start thinking about the required mindset because you need to be prepared.

Leadership is personal. You will make your own mark in your own way. It is important, however, to learn not only from your own journey, but also from those of others, who can provide hard-earned wisdom and experience.

I have taken some time to consider what to share with you in this part. Some of it may seem irrelevant for now, but when you're in a leadership role and you come back to read it, I promise you it will make a lot of sense.

I am writing this on a sunny Saturday afternoon and there is nothing I would rather be doing than sharing my thoughts on leadership to help you prepare for a big life.

CHAPTER 21

SETTING PRIORITIES

For the first six to 12 months in a role, your overarching priority should be to consistently fulfil all that is required of you to the best of your ability. Listen carefully and possess an obvious appetite for outdoing your own performance on every task.

Once you move beyond that period, you can start thinking about your priorities from a far more holistic point of view. Key to this is gaining an understanding of the key pillars of your organisation's corporate plan (typically available on the company website). What you are looking to do is identify how your day-to-day activities contribute to the organisation's strategic goals. Look at your priorities and ask whether they are in line with or really enhancing these strategic goals. If not, perhaps it is time to review, reprioritise or have a discussion with your manager.

This analysis is a worthwhile exercise as you move towards leadership positions where your priorities will be increasingly framed by the strategic directions of the business. Understanding the big game of the business—its primary objectives, why they're important and the strategy behind reaching them—will stand you in good stead for that day you do become a leader.

Mapping your priorities to and framing your conversations around the strategic pillars will also help you build your case for promotion. People will likely recognise and respect the fact that you have a firm grip on what the business is trying to achieve.

I will give you an example. When I was appointed CEO of CPA Australia, the overarching strategic objective we set for the business was to become the best member services organisation in the world. Therefore, I expect each department and staff member to prioritise this objective in everything they do. What they do each day should be feeding into this objective. When we review our performance at year's end, I expect everyone to articulate how their work has specifically contributed to our objective, our benchmark. So having a clear understanding of how your role feeds into the bigger picture is important.

If you remain unsure, speak to your manager. Find out his or her priorities, which should be in line with key business objectives, and then map those against your own responsibilities. Ensuring your priorities are in line with your direct manager's objectives and responsibilities is an essential guide for your own prioritisation.

Naturally, your manager's priorities will change over time. So, during meetings or general conversations, always listen to what they are talking about in terms of their own workload. Are they working on a project that has an extremely tight deadline? Has an unexpected project arisen and you know they already have a lot on their plate? Do they look or sound a bit stressed? If so, take the initiative to offer your assistance before they ask for it. Even if they decline, they will appreciate your willingness to help and ability to observe.

Thinking laterally is also useful. What are the other departments you are working with prioritising? Are you in a position to assist? Are they relying on you? Remember, sometimes their priorities can help you recognise and organise your own.

MAKE IT HAPPEN: HOW TO SET PRIORITIES
The following provides well-tested techniques for setting priorities.

Prioritise issues in your job description
While completing all your tasks is essential, start by studying your job description and highlighting those activities that most obviously matter to the overall direction of the business. Maintain a keen eye on those activities.

Work out when time can be a friend

Many people claim to have no time, yet we often hear the saying, 'If you want something done, ask a busy person to do it.' The busiest people are often so because they can be relied on to get the job done. This means you need to learn how to have time on your side where possible. A good exercise to help you prepare for an increased workload is to measure the time each of your regular tasks take to complete. Aim to reduce the duration each time, ensuring it is not at the expense of quality outputs. Setting a personal deadline to work towards can be effective in this.

Understand the importance of order

Now that you have refined your timings, be more thoughtful about whether you are undertaking your tasks in the appropriate priority order. A properly ordered routine will almost certainly guarantee you a strong reputation in the minds of your colleagues and manager. This capacity is also often an early sign that you have the ability to multi-task—a key skill in leadership.

Quotable quote from Alex

I have every confidence your passion is out there for you to find, and you just have to believe it, fight for it and persist in your search if you have to. Nothing great comes easily, unless you are unlucky enough for it to happen so.

Expect the unexpected

Always remember that no matter how organised you might become, anything can happen, at any time. If an unforseen priority issue arises, be willing and flexible enough to attend to it immediately. This is a real opportunity to promote something different about you—the ability to perform under pressure and uncertainty. Do not let your organised focus blind you to dealing with unexpected big issues.

Live with the burden of success

The better you become at prioritising, the more in demand you will likely become. People will observe your efficiency and notice your broader understanding of the business. They will want in on your apparent confidence and success, so expect additional requests to come your way. Helping others with additional work requests is a positive action, but at times your existing workload will not permit anything extra and you'll have to say 'no'. This can be difficult (see chapter 19 for more), but my prediction is you will become good at this once you've said 'yes' too often.

Review and prepare

Until you become more experienced, get into the daily habit of critiquing your outcomes and performance. Short moments of reflection are invaluable in assessing your own development. Always plan for tomorrow's activities and be a step ahead at all times.

DON'T FORGET

Here are some tips for setting priorities:

- identify how your day-to-day activities contribute to the organisation's strategic goals
- ensure your priorities are in line with your direct manager's objectives and responsibilities
- keep in mind priorities can be disrupted without notice—be aware and flexible
- speak with your manager about adjusting priorities if in doubt—avoid making assumptions.

Get ahead of the pack

To really be ahead of the pack when setting priorities, follow these tips:

- *Add it up:* An article recently published in *The Sydney Morning Herald* stated that workers spend 61 per cent of their day lost in emails and not actually achieving the outcomes they had originally set out to do. Don't let this be you! Prioritise your tasks and have a set time each day—perhaps thirty minutes mid-morning and mid-afternoon—when you go through and respond to your emails.

- *Ask yourself:* Can you at this very moment outline the pillars of your business's strategy, vision and mission? If you can't, what is the broad frame from which you are setting your priorities?

Meet the mentee: Liam Smith

University of Canberra student Liam Smith has a long-term goal: to be the CEO of a financial services company. But realising that was his dream was not an overnight process.

Liam was just about to graduate with a Bachelor of Commerce, majoring in accounting, which was what got him thinking seriously about what kind of career he wanted in the future.

'The first time I got to chat with Alex we spoke about having the confidence to go out there and figure out what I want from life without caring if I come up short or miss my targets for any particular goal because you can always try again,' Liam said.

Alex encouraged Liam to think about the direction he wanted his career to move in—what priorities he would need to set in order to achieve his goals. Alex said Liam should focus on the number one priority: seeking out opportunities to learn and gain experience.

'For me, it was all about taking the time to sit down and work out where I would like to be, and what I wanted. Just to focus on where I want to get to, then making a plan for that and putting it in to action,' said Liam.

This advice helped Liam to secure two industry placements—a contract role at the National Australia Bank (NAB) that he is completing during his final year of study, and a graduate role at EY, which will begin after Liam graduates. Recently, Liam was also awarded a scholarship to spend a month studying international business in China.

Liam and Alex spoke a lot about setting aside time to plan and set goals, rather than waiting for ideas to manifest on their own. They focused on the importance of new ideas and of delegating the time to generate ideas.

Liam took Alex's advice on board and put together a five-year plan for his career, identifying the different things he would need to prioritise in his daily routine to be successful in his plan.

According to Liam, Alex's advice really reinforced the idea that no-one is going to just hand you opportunities. 'You have to put your best foot forward by knowing exactly what you want. You have to do what is necessary to grab them yourself.'

CHAPTER 22

THE IMPORTANCE OF DELEGATING

During the early stages of your career, you will likely become accustomed to people expecting you to do everything yourself. A manager allocated you a task and you would have fulfilled it from beginning to end. Understand this means you will likely develop a sense of full control over the manner in which you undertake your duties. Ironically, this sense of full control is almost the opposite to what you will feel in leadership, particularly in the early days.

Here is why. While on the surface delegation sounds like a luxury, finding the ability to do so with confidence is much tougher than you might think. This is because you're entrusting someone to complete a task that you are ultimately responsible for. Effectively, you're handing them your reputation to manage. This transition from individual ownership to shared ownership is something I have seen countless young leaders struggle to come to grips with. To be honest, some never do.

So a tough and often ongoing lesson in leadership is learning how to let go. The more senior you become, the greater the breadth of responsibilities you will be accountable for, so it will be impossible for you to be involved in every stage of every process. In leadership, a sense of total control no longer exists. This has to be replaced with a sense of total trust.

Ineffectual delegation is a common reason people give up on leadership. They just can't let go. Maintaining this control is also disheartening for staff members because they're not being delegated enough responsibility. Know that this can affect the whole team's morale.

Delegation is not about outsourcing tasks because it's simply convenient or because you don't like them. In order to progress yourself, you need to help others progress, so delegate with that in mind.

But what about if things do go wrong? Blaming a colleague for a poor outcome is unacceptable leadership form. Although you no longer have a hawk-like focus on every stage of every project, it is still your responsibility. You will need to monitor things better next time. Welcome to the sometimes-bitter taste of leadership.

Empowering others with responsibility is a constant process that you will become more attuned to through working with various people. It will, however, always remain a great challenge. The right person is not always the most obvious and colleagues do not always measure up to their job titles.

This is why you need to constantly listen and observe. How did the person you delegated a particular task to cope? Did they come across as eager or reluctant to take it on? Were they obviously stressed under the weight of pressure? Did they constantly seek reassurance? Did their final product meet an acceptable standard? Consistently finding the answers to these sorts of questions will help you identify where the person's key strengths and weaknesses lie, because this is invaluable intelligence for future delegation.

Identifying and playing to people's strengths is key to efficiency and successful outcomes. For instance, perhaps a person proves to be adept at writing, so, wherever possible, you allocate work to them where written communication is fundamental to a successful outcome.

Delegating such complementary tasks to people will not always be possible, however. As I discuss in chapter 18, like you, the delegate will need to complete tasks they find unfavourable and you will need them to suck it up. Open communication is essential during these circumstances. Let them know that you understand the task might be less than enjoyable, but emphasise its importance to your collective objectives. Perhaps even run through the business' strategic priorities and show them where the task factors into it. This should help instil in them a sense of purpose and motivation. If they continue to fall short, take them aside and deliver some constructive advice so that they are clear about your expectations and what they need to work on.

On the flip side, the person might be a superstar, producing a quality of work perhaps better than you used to produce on the same task. Do not let intimidation or self-doubt threaten you, and do recognise their talents and delegate them more duties. Encourage them and see how they respond. Surrounding yourself with talented people will never hurt you.

As a CEO, I am constantly looking to hire people who are smarter than me. I want the best people on my team. So do not feel threatened by talent, embrace it. Know that it is your job as the leader to mobilise them towards an objective. Their success is your success and it is a reflection of your ability to bring out the best in people.

MAKE IT HAPPEN: HOW TO DELEGATE

Being organised is hard if you insist on doing everything yourself. Delegating to others is not only helpful but also crucial to your success. If letting go isn't quite your strong suit, follow these tips to learn how to delegate effectively.

Know your people

Remember, delegation is about trust. To build trust with a person you need to know them. Everyone has strengths and weaknesses. Understand their place within the team and factor their strengths and weaknesses in when assigning tasks. Wherever possible seek to play to a person's strengths.

Set expectations

After delegating duties, make sure the person you appoint understands what is required and has all the tools necessary to complete the task. Ensure you offer them the opportunity to ask any further questions as required.

Remain responsible

Always remind your colleagues that you will take full and final responsibility for the tasks assigned. Emphasise the importance of their delegation to the team. Ensure you match the responsibility you assign with the person's authority and capability.

Be opportunistic

If issues become increasingly complex, do not be afraid to bring the team together, or obtain external advice. Having a team work on an issue together can prove both efficient and positive for staff morale.

Quotable quote from Alex

A tough and often ongoing lesson in leadership is learning how to let go. The more senior you become, the greater the breadth of responsibilities you will be accountable for, so it will be impossible for you to be involved in every stage of every process. In leadership, a sense of total control no longer exists. This has to be replaced with a sense of total trust.

Empower your team

The more you trust, empower and support your team, the quicker they should learn and advance their skills. Be aware, however, that empowerment has interesting implications. For some, it generates energy and drive; for others, it creates uncertainty or a fear of failure. Always keep a close eye on people's body language as they progress towards the goal.

Communicate and acknowledge

Make sure you communicate clearly when giving instructions to your team. When you are assigning a task, provide a deadline and define your expectations. Be even-handed and consistent with your acknowledgements.

Staff need to understand that you are equally comfortable in recognising excellent performance or poor performance. People respect and trust consistent behaviour.

Do not micromanage

A micromanager is someone who can't let go. They hover around colleagues, always checking on the progress of delegated activities. These types of managers are unable to distinguish between the big picture issues and day-to-day operations.

Besides distracting yourself from more senior business priorities, you will be doing the delegate a disservice if you're consistently breathing down their neck. Like you, they're also trying to build their brand and enhance their learning, and this will not be possible if they are constantly working in your shadow.

Be part of the team

Never delegate something you are not willing to do yourself because that is the fastest way to lose the respect of your team. Take opportunities to lend a hand, provide some guidance or share a responsibility.

Concern yourself with what is being ultimately accomplished, rather than detailing how the work should be done. Allow the person to control his or her own methods and processes. This will build trust.

DON'T FORGET

Here are points to remember when delegating effectively:

- delegation is not about outsourcing tasks because it's convenient or that you don't like them—it's about achieving results efficiently
- play to people's strengths
- the task you've delegated is still your ultimate responsibility
- specific communication of your expectations is imperative.

Get ahead of the pack

Here's how to take your delegating skills to the next level:

- *Do it:* Create a 'delegation matrix' that will help you keep track of tasks, deadlines and accountabilities. This is imperative in managing the delegation process towards successful outcomes.

- *Ask yourself:* What is holding you back from delegating responsibility? Fear of losing control? Not getting credit? Find out what it is and work on it! The biggest barrier to effective delegation is often you. In order to be a great leader, you must overcome your anxieties about trusting others.

Meet the mentee: Brooke Jennings

Brooke Jennings knows firsthand the importance of delegating effectively in her university and work life. For the last six years, the twenty-six year old has been not only working full-time in the finance department of one of Australia's biggest producers of hygiene and cleaning products, but also studying part-time at the University of Newcastle.

Brooke admitted that early on she had trouble delegating tasks to colleagues, or to fellow students when she needed to complete a university group assignment—so she sought some advice from Alex about effective delegation.

'It was such an inspiring session and the answers I received from Alex Malley really helped to bridge the gap between my university and work life, especially when it came to delegating tasks,' said Brooke.

She believes the best piece of advice she received was about the importance of finding out people's strengths and delegating specific tasks to them. This advice has provided guidance for both her group university assignments and also at work.

'Whenever I have a tough work project due, I now have the skills to effectively delegate jobs to my other team members,' Brooke said.

'For example, two people at my work are a lot better at using a particular type of software than me. So if I am given a massive job to do, I'll ask them to get the basic information from the software for me and ask them for help if I can't interpret the data.'

Brooke said she has learnt that if you want to be successful in your career, you need to be an effective delegator and trust that people will get the job done. Not only does this ensure you help to reach your organisation's targets, but you can also learn a lot from other people this way and achieve your own personal goals.

'Learning how to delegate effectively is a good step towards achieving a positive result for everyone. In the end, everyone wants to get a job finished. That is what a good team does, so it's all about using each team member effectively.'

CHAPTER 23

BUILDING YOUR LEADERSHIP CONFIDENCE

You can make confidence a discipline. It is about finding an inner belief that you are capable of handling different situations and knowing that the world is not going to end if you make a mistake or do not produce a desired outcome.

Confidence is a state of mind that you can cultivate from various experiences. The secret is to get into the habit of confronting difficult circumstances. As they say in the classics: you will win some and you will lose some. However, the experience of working through difficult situations will build your self-belief, and this will become your leadership foundation.

With enough practice, encountering a difficult situation is like watching an action replay. Having dealt with difficult situations before, the benefit is that you will know how to fix an issue, not because you are the smartest person in the room, but because you have been there before and you have learnt from it. Often, someone you perceive as wise and confident is simply someone who's been exposed to a similar problem before. With the right attitude of being willing to deal with difficult circumstances, you will be that person.

Wisdom is a collection of experiences, so it makes sense to start collecting them now.

No-one is going to build your confidence for you because that is your job. Remember the black box concept I introduced you to back in chapter 5? That place inside of you where you lock away all the confidence and satisfaction you have derived from your various achievements? Call upon these feelings when confronted by future challenges during your ascent up the career ladder. Ironically, those challenges may not come from others, but from you because you may lack the maturity to face certain realities.

For instance, when you are young and inexperienced, the need to be liked by others can be all-consuming. Whereas when you seek a leadership role, you have to be very clear in the fact that leadership is about respect, not popularity. Leadership can be a very lonely place and it is even lonelier if you do not keep the confidence you have earned. Take every opportunity to be the one to volunteer to lead a difficult project, break bad news or deal with a difficult staff matter. All such experiences will teach you how irrelevant popularity is in the wonderful world of leadership.

Always—but always—separate your personal identity from your title. Young leaders can get carried away by their position and the authority that goes with it. This is a big mistake. At all times, remember who you are, stay true to yourself and, no matter how hard you work and may love your role, remember it is not what defines you as person. If you keep this principle at the forefront of your mind, your confidence will grow and stay strong, even if one day that role is taken from you, either fairly or unfairly.

And so if that job is lost, or your title is removed, it is only a temporary setback. Learn from the experience, brush yourself off and get back in the game. The pain of such circumstances is much more manageable when you have kept separate your personal identity, and your confidence, from your title. The passion to achieve in an area of great interest is what matters, not the description of your public title.

MAKE IT HAPPEN: BUILDING CONFIDENCE IN YOURSELF AS A LEADER

The following outlines some of the attributes you need to build within yourself to have confidence as a leader.

Courage

Like most things in life, fear can become a habit. Fear for some people is a default setting that provides them with a convenient internal excuse for not stretching themselves. For others, a genuine concern may exist simply because they fear failure or do not want to disappoint someone else. In a work situation, neither case is warranted.

In my view, life is measured by the stretch involved, not by the comfort gained.

A confident leader has worked through the issues of fear and insecurity. They have been through the moments of looking in the mirror and wondering whether they have the courage to face the challenge. These moments are special, the highlights that more often than not bring confidence to the fore. I want you to want those moments and stretch your life beyond anything you currently envisage. I know you can.

Attitude

If you're lucky enough to have your health and the opportunity to have a full life, you have every reason to be confident and grateful. If you take that attitude and appreciate all that comes your way, nothing is stopping you having a positive life. Always fall back on this attitude when things don't go your way. Remember, there is always someone worse off than you. Your attitude defines your life.

Quotable quote from Alex

Wisdom is a collection of experiences, so it makes sense to start collecting them now.

Resilience

When things go wrong, understand that these are great moments because they will teach you about yourself and your strength of character. The more you test yourself, the more you will discover how truly resilient you can be.

Grace after rejection

As you mature, you will likely recognise many of the reasons for personal rejection are superficial and unnecessary. Focus on the basics—ensure you are polite, respectful and do the best you can in all you do. If after that people for some reason reject you, accept that as a part of life and maintain your values and good grace. By all means, seek clarification if you wish to but remember you can't always change people's attitude towards you.

Continuous improvement

Frame your life on continuous improvement. Whether you face rejection or you have made a mistake, ensure you absorb the lesson. Confidence is earned by a sense of achievement, and a learning experience in a difficult circumstance is exactly that. If you adopt the principle of continuous improvement, before too long you will be encouraging others to learn something every day of their life, too.

DON'T FORGET

Keep in mind these points to help build your confidence as a leader:

- confronting challenges, rather than shying away from them, will make you stronger
- learn from negative experiences, rather than being disheartened by them
- fearing failure is a waste of time and energy—don't hold yourself back
- when you make a mistake or face rejection, focus on how you can improve, and then make it happen.

Get ahead of the pack

Follow these tips to really build and maintain your leadership confidence:

- *Add it up:* Confidence is mostly learned. According to *Forbes* magazine, people with a healthy self-esteem perform at their best and treat others with respect. They also report that the most common cause of entrepreneur failure is giving up too early—resilience matters.

- *Ask yourself:* What experiences are you initiating that are taking you on your continuous improvement path? You should be able to think of examples from your work and private life. What are they?

Meet the mentee: Kaylah Almanro

At the age of twenty-four, Kaylah Almanro was juggling looking after a newborn daughter with full-time study at the University of Western Sydney and a part-time job. As a result, she began to question whether she could successfully manage everything in her schedule. She felt as though her attention was spread so thin that her self-confidence began to wane.

Kaylah met with Alex and he reminded her that everything she had achieved so far showed great strength, talent and management ability. He also pointed out that Kaylah obviously possessed an inner strength that enabled her to keep up with her extremely demanding lifestyle.

'Straightaway Alex was able to relate with me on a personal level. I think through speaking with me he was able to notice that my professional confidence wasn't really there yet,' said Kaylah. 'Because of that he gave me a lot of advice about building self-confidence.

'Thinking that someone at Alex's level could have faith in me and see good qualities in me, made me realise I should be able to see those qualities in myself.'

Kaylah says that having the CEO of a large organisation shed some light on the skills and personality traits she had displayed during her recent challenges was enlightening to her.

'It's so easy to be hard on yourself and to look past your own achievements. When I was speaking to Alex, I started to see that I do know more, and am capable of more than I realise,' she said.

Kaylah learnt that her journey and situation contributed to the value she would bring to professional roles in the future, even if she had not had the same experiences as other young professionals.

'Alex spoke to me about how everyone starting out in their career is in the same situation of being a bit nervous, but how I'm the one who got myself to the point I was at, which is something to be proud of. It was just a real confidence booster,' Kaylah said.

Two years after their meeting, Kaylah has worked her way from receptionist to senior accountant at a medium-sized public practice firm in Sydney. She said that when she first started interacting with clients as an accountant she was extremely nervous.

'It was very obvious when I first started meeting with clients that I was very nervous and shy. So I had to slow it down and tell myself everything would be fine and to remind myself to have more confidence,' said Kaylah.

Pacing herself when taking on challenges helps Kaylah to avoid being flustered or feeling stressed, which helps her to maintain her self-confidence. She says doing so helps her to be sure she hasn't forgotten or missed anything and, as a result, she can be sure that she has done a great job.

Kaylah plans to use her new-found confidence to study for her CPA designation and to obtain her MBA. She hopes to one day start her own accounting firm.

CHAPTER 24

THE WORK–LIFE BALANCE MYTH

Most of us spend more time at work than anywhere else. Therefore, doesn't it make sense to love what you do?

As I wrote in the introduction to Part V, make working in a field you are passionate about your number one priority. By doing this you will likely reduce any pressure you may place on yourself to achieve the 'right' work–life balance—whatever that is...

To me, work–life balance is a fallacy. It is an unnecessary distraction. I listen to people talk about it as if it is some sort of symmetrical model: that a certain percentage of your day should be allocated to your professional life, and the other to life outside of work. Some people spend their whole careers trying to find the 'perfect balance', only to become frustrated or resentful when they are unable to achieve it. So many elements of professional life are out of your control and demand your time and energy, particularly as you become more senior. Finding a balance—although a nice ideal—to me is a misguided focus.

The term 'work–life balance' should be substituted with 'work–life quality'. Make the moments at work and during your personal time really count. Live in the moment.

I have never spent less time with my family than I do today. The demands of my role require me to be in a multitude of places both mentally and geographically. Rather than desiring to spend more time with my loved ones—which, of course, I'd value greatly—I accept that at this stage of my life it is difficult to achieve. I make sure, however, that the time we do have together is undivided. It is quality. I have become much better at living in the moment. You should try it. It is effective.

It is also important to make time for yourself, to find a way to unwind.

No matter what part of the world I am in, every day I go for an early morning walk. The phone is off and I have at least an hour alone with my thoughts. This makes me a much better performer. So I encourage you to find ways to incorporate time for yourself into your daily routine.

MAKE IT HAPPEN: ACHIEVING WORK–LIFE QUALITY

Instead of focusing on work–life balance, in the following sections I take you through how to achieve work–life quality, by appreciating three stages of your working life.

Stage one

When you start full-time employment it is a dramatic experience—whether that be positive or negative. To move from school or university to a professional workplace is a significant change of pace and lifestyle. In the rumble of trying to come to grips with your new world, simply focus on getting used to a work environment and all that it is. Outside of work, do what you have always done—enjoy every moment, including sharing your newly formed perspectives and experiences with friends and relatives. At this stage of your career, you will likely keep the two worlds relatively separate.

Stage two

In later years, with the right attitude and having followed your passions, your job is likely to become something you enjoy and look forward to. This is where you will begin to notice a blurring of the lines between professional and personal life. Being at work interacting with your colleagues will seem a combination of both aspects of your life. Your work is adding to the quality of your life. A change has taken place, often without you noticing. This is where you should begin to think about the quality of each moment, whether at work or with family and friends.

Quotable quote from Alex

Make working in a field you are passionate about your number one priority. By doing this you will likely reduce any pressure you may place on yourself to achieve the 'right' work–life balance.

Stage three

You have reached the senior post in an organisation. Work is demanding even more of your time and attention. It is providing you with challenges, fulfilment and quality relationships. It is a way of life. Like every stage in the work–life quality progression, you need to be aware of the changes taking place. In these scenarios, balance no longer becomes the issue. You have to accept that you have been empowered to do great things with your team. The objective now becomes the extraction of quality out of every moment of your life, whether that is professional or personal. It will heighten your appreciation of both.

DON'T FORGET

Here's what to focus on when looking to achieve work–life quality:

- find a vocation you're truly passionate about—it may take time, but it's worth it
- make the time you spend in your personal and professional worlds really count

- no matter how busy you are, there will always be opportunities to make time for yourself—and finding ways to fit those moments into your routine will make you a better performer

- when you are busy, remember: there are likely many other people out there who'd love to have your opportunity, so you should appreciate it at all times.

Get ahead of the pack

Ramp your efforts up and focus on your work–life quality with the following:

- *Do it:* Healthy body, healthy mind—even though you're busy, finding the time for daily exercise is essential.

- *Find out more:* Visit thenakedceo.com for tips and further reading.

Meet the mentee: Carys Chan

Carys Chan completed her undergraduate studies at Australian National University. With a dream of obtaining her PhD, Carys did not know whether to start work and gain some real-world experience before continuing in academia, or to obtain her PhD ahead of joining the workforce.

Carys had always had concerns about developing a work–life balance for her prospective career. She wanted to develop a fulfilling career in an area that she felt passionate about, but she didn't want her dedication to her vocation to affect her personal life.

Carys reached out to Alex for some advice.

Alex said that few people achieve a perfect balance between their work and their personal life. Inevitably, work would occupy a significant portion of her time, so, pursuing a career in a field she is passionate about should be her overarching priority.

'The fact is that achieving great things professionally doesn't always come with perfect symmetry and balance between one aspect of life or another,' said Alex. 'There will be some times in your life when you just give everything you have to one particular activity, and a lot of the time that activity will be work.'

Alex went on to say that people should work towards achieving work–life quality.

'Alex told me that you have to monitor yourself and make sure that even though there will always be times of imbalance when you're pursuing your career goals, you should always make sure that you're at least in contact in some way with your family and friends in a way that brings you comfort and happiness,' Carys said.

Off the back of her meeting with Alex, Carys developed a fresh approach to effectively combining her work and personal life, as well as deciding to follow her passion—studying for her PhD. She is now completing her academic exploration into the psychology of increasing the happiness and efficiency of workforces.

Carys dreams of developing and implementing training and workshop programs to help people to build confidence and clarity in effectively managing their workloads and their lifestyles. She hopes that she will be able to unlock the secret to empowering workers to be more efficient and content at work, and happier at home.

Carys aspires to complete her PhD studies and then start a career in the world of corporate human resources, where she can implement her work–life efficiency program and help others to be happier in their work and in their personal lives. She acknowledges that a lot of work is ahead of her, but she'll be making sure to pay attention to the findings of her own research in order to maintain her own happiness and work–life integration.

CHAPTER 25

LEADERSHIP—IT'S PERSONAL

Many people ask me how I define a quality leader. For me, in its most simple terms, a leader is someone who can mobilise people towards a vision.

It is fascinating that some leaders ooze charisma, whereas others possess no look of command or presence, but, somehow, they also inspire people. So don't assume mobilising people means you have to pull out a trumpet and blow it. Rather, mobilising people is about developing your own style, learning about the people you lead, being authentic and creating a positive belief in the journey ahead.

The best thing you can do early on in leadership is to adopt the principle of 'do as I do', rather than 'do as I say'. Your influence will be enhanced if you're willing to roll up your sleeves and are prepared to help on the most menial tasks.

Let me share an example of this principle in action. My father owned a furniture business, managing about fifty employees. As a child I would often visit Dad at work, where I'd find him sanding pieces of furniture alongside the apprentices. At the time I had no concept of why he was doing that—he was the boss, after all. The older I became, the more I started to realise that he was doing it because if you stand shoulder to shoulder with those you are leading, their level of respect and willingness to come with you will grow. They will not think you believe you are above the 'lowly tasks'. You will have pressing responsibilities of a different nature so will not always have time to do this, but early on in your leadership tenure I suggest you find the time to do it.

Only in more recent years can I see many of the lessons my father offered me but, at the time, was too young to appreciate. The ongoing story of humankind, you might say. This book aims to break that cycle. By sharing honest advice and experience I hope it sets you on your way to a big life.

By now you have a sense of who I am, my values and the fondness with which I reflect on my many mistakes. My career, like most, has had highs and lows. Over time I have developed philosophies that have framed my leadership approach. Your journey will be different, as might be your approach. While I wish you great success, promise me that you will learn during the tough times and fight back against what might, at the time, seem like insurmountable challenges. They will be the diamond learning moments that you will cherish and they will help you to form your own leadership philosophies.

MAKE IT HAPPEN: DEVELOPING YOUR OWN LEADERSHIP STYLE

My leadership journey to date has been as exciting as it has been challenging. I share some learnings and philosophies in the following sections.

Listen and observe

When you first accept a leadership position, you might be tempted to make immediate changes to established processes. While I applaud this enthusiasm, ensure you don't make rushed decisions.

It is a good idea during the first few months of the role to pay close attention to existing processes, relationships and issues. Listen and observe as much as you can. Informal conversations can be incredibly illuminating.

When you feel you have an understanding of core issues, you can then begin to make informed decisions. Having ongoing discussions with staff about the directions you wish to take is important, carefully explaining why you have come to such conclusions.

Work hard and consistently to understand the personality skills mix that you have around you. In order to bring out the best in people, you first need to identify their strengths and weaknesses, what motivates and frustrates them, because this will influence your leadership impact.

Listening and observing is a 24/7 trait for great leaders.

Be authentic

Leaders who are authentic have a deeper and more sustainable impact on those around them. People have great respect and trust for those who have the courage to be themselves no matter what their rank. By being yourself, you don't risk wasting your energies on pretending to be someone you are not.

Building trust through an authentic approach is imperative. Be yourself.

Practise self-awareness

A key aspect of leadership requires you to have a heightened awareness of how your behaviour and actions affect others. In reality, no-one will tell you—you have to work it out. That can take time.

When I was a younger I learnt the hard way. My view of myself was very different to how others perceived me. This provoked conflict. I was simply unaware of the impact my behaviour was having on others. So understand that one of the most important qualities of a genuine leader is unwavering self-awareness—a consistent consciousness of what sort of impact you're having on everyone you deal with. If you have never really thought about how you might appear in the minds of others, I recommend you start doing so.

If you can marry your self-awareness with other people's perceptions so that they are consistent, one in the same, you're on your way to a big future. Self-awareness should become a permanent outlook.

A life without self-awareness is stunted.

> ## Quotable quote from Alex
>
> It is fascinating that some leaders ooze charisma, whereas others possess no look of command or presence, but, somehow, they also inspire people. So don't assume mobilising people means you have to pull out a trumpet and blow it. Rather, mobilising people is about developing your own style, learning about the people you lead, being authentic and creating a positive belief in the journey ahead.

Show strength and empathy

Ironically, there is no greater strength than the expression of empathy. In leadership, always take the opportunity to exhibit your understanding when a colleague faces difficult times—whether that be as a result of their own actions or not. A moment of kindness when a person is vulnerable can present a profound opportunity to recast a relationship and allow confidence to be built or rebuilt.

A timely kindness can turn a person's life around.

Remember it's not about the title

The most effective leaders are not defined by their own success or the title they hold. On many occasions you see a person's life unravel when they lose their leadership role. This is often because they have unwittingly allowed their title to be their identity and provider of confidence. Throughout your life, always ensure that you don't align your identity to your title. Not only will doing so make you more tentative in conducting your responsibilities, but you'll also be shattered if the title is taken away.

Your role should not define you.

Earn the right to influence

For some, influence is a skill that develops slowly through multiple experiences; whereas for others, it is a totally natural process. This latter group, in their early years at least, is at great personal risk because their influencing capacity is far more developed than their maturity.

I fell within this latter group when I was a young professional and was elevated into a position of great influence far sooner than I should've been. Consequently, I made some big mistakes—like going over people's heads, and wielding my influence irresponsibly and with little regard for how I was impacting on people. This stirred a negative backlash towards me from many people in the business and my ability to influence was crushed as a result.

So do not be in a rush to influence. People will follow and be open to your recommended ideas and direction if you earn their trust through consistent performance and an authentic nature.

Take time to earn the right to influence.

Listen to your instinct

One of the greatest attributes of many people is their instinct—their feel for a situation or what they inherently believe in. Like most things, you must exercise it to preserve its value. Most young people have good instinct but somehow let it go when they begin to navigate workplace life. Hold on to it, because it's the one thing you really can count on in leadership and in life.

When it comes to making decisions, some leaders listen to their instinct; others often ignore it, instead deferring the decision to others. Remember, at the core of leadership is decision-making.

While informing your decisions is important, sometimes your instinct will tell you to ignore the advice and take a different tack. In your leadership journey these moments will arise so trust your judgement.

In the toughest of times your instinct can be your best friend.

Possess the courage to fail

At the core of many issues in business and life is the fear of failure. It has never been more prevalent than in today's world. Organisations, like society, need inspired leadership. This is about stretching the boundaries, finding new frontiers and having the courage to fail in the quest to achieve such goals.

When you ask people to follow you, you must exhibit the traits that you require in them. They will always observe your behaviour, looking for consistency, resilience and courage. Look for the moment to embrace a tough challenge rather than walk away from it, because this can begin to create a culture of momentum and belief.

Courage is built from the top down.

Show vision

In an organisation, vision is deemed to be a collective direction. In truth, vision must be energised, owned and driven by the leader. They must convert the vision to an inspiring story worth hearing and achieving. It must be aspirational to the extent that it stretches the team and challenges the individual.

Authentic belief in the vision underpins the journey to success.

Communicate effectively

A great leader converses at all levels, using all channels available. The leader's tone and body language is all important in defining the culture of the organisation.

In the modern era, we have the challenges of globalisation and complexity. Communication skills have never been more important in bringing people together in an ever-expanding world.

My cultural objective in leadership is to build a personable and hospitable environment. This requires sensitivity towards others, respectful communication and encouragement to succeed. However, my most powerful communication weapons remain a kind word and a handwritten note—they're personal.

The simple things in life matter the most.

CONCLUSION

A BIG LIFE

I do recall with a smile the beginning of The Naked CEO journey when people told me, 'Alex, you're a CEO, not a teacher anymore.'

You can never stop being a teacher. It is the core responsibility of a leader. The issue today, at least in my mind, is that we talk a lot about mentoring and teaching but it's not matched by action in the business world.

This book is a promise I made to myself when I first sat in a lecture theatre at university, wondering how I was possibly going to move from the class to this thing called 'the real world'. It took me a long time to master 'the real world' and I could have done with some help. This book is designed to guide and shorten your mastery journey.

It is okay to dream about a big life—one that is lived on your terms, breathes your passion and inspires others. That big life, however, does not come easy. It requires unstinting resolve, persistence and a willingness to suck it up along the way. Whether during the tough moments, or the exhilarating ones, always stay true to you. I want you to promise me that when you get to your mountain top that nothing is different about you that your friends or family can see, other than you are a lot wiser for your journey.

Make every mistake count and force yourself to laugh in the toughest of times. I promise, everything eventually seems smaller than it did at the time. Earn your confidence, nurture it, and then help to build it in others. Do not abandon it when others (rightly or wrongly) lose a little faith in you. You can always rebuild relationships by maintaining an open and positive mind.

Unless you're comfortable with your own journey, you're unlikely to truly help others on theirs. **In some ways you've got to be selfish before you can be truly generous.** Often you can only be of real benefit to others when you understand your own true value. The aim is to be comfortable in your own skin. It's a worthwhile ambition.

Be willing to ride the roller-coaster that is your journey with a white-knuckle grip and a courage to fail in getting there. It took me too long to commit to my journey and I challenge you to be faster and better than me in owning your adventure. This book is my commitment to helping you along the way.

And I meant what I wrote in the prologue—if you have any questions about your career after reading this book, contact me via the Ask Alex section at thenakedceo.com and I will personally respond via video.

Now go and find your big life.

INDEX

accountability, importance of 19
Almanro, Kaylah 200–201
Annetta, Rosalaura 53
attire, workplace 96
attitude, benefits of having
   the right 131–132
authenticity
   —benefits of 5
   —how to act with 6–10
   —in leadership 196, 211
   —in negotiation 124–125
   —influence and 11
   —networking and 59

Bernhardt, Emma-Jaye
   129–130
bosses, establishing rapport
   with 102
branding yourself 6, 8–9
   —business cards and 58
   —LinkedIn and 68
business cards 58

career paths, changing 18
Chan, Carys 207–208
communication
   —developing skills for good
   93–94

—key to effective 91–92
—leadership and 214
comparing self with others 7
confidence
   —building 36, 55, 195–196
   —gratitude and 38–39
   —knowledge and 38
   —leadership and 196–199
   —momentum and 38
   —past experiences and 37
   —preserving 35–36
   —procrastination and
   38–39
   —risk-taking and 36
cover letters 75

deadlines, importance of
   meeting 136
delegation 187–192
   —leadership and 187
   —trust and 189
disorganisation, consequences
   of 135
dreams 14
Durrani, Waqas 100

embarrassment 2
energy, best use of 5–6

failure
—fear of 25, 142
—leadership and 214
fear 2
—consequences of 144
—dealing with 196–197
—of failure 25, 142
flexibility, goals and 16

Garthwaite, Damian 77–78
goals
—defining and achieving
15–17
—setting 184
Green, Alistair 173–174

honesty 7–8

icebreakers 103–104
impression, making a good
—in networking 59–60
—on your first day at work
97
—with colleagues 102–105
influence 125–128
—authenticity and 11
—building 123
—gaining through
storytelling 124, 127
—leadership and 213
insights
—benefits of 28
—breaking habits to gain
30–31
—changing environment to
gain 29
—finding 28–29
—free writing to gain 29
—observation and 30

instincts
—leadership and 213
—listening to your 9–10
interpersonal skills
—building 151–152
—importance of 115
interviews
—preparing for 81–83
—succeeding in 83–86
—what interviewers are
looking for in 79–80

Jakate, Anand 18
Jennings, Brooke 193–194
jobs
—reasons to leave 168–169
—that are a bad fit, dealing
with 149–153
—working out whether to
leave 169–171
journaling, building self-
awareness through 10

Kirby, Rhiannon 139–140

leadership
—blaming others in 188
—confidence and 196–199
—delegation and 187
—developing your style of
210–214
—getting on the track to
175
—key skills of 136, 181
—passion and 177
—qualities of 115, 209
—understanding your
motivation towards
177

learning
—from listening to others 59
—from mistakes 19–20
—from past experiences 37
—the power of continuous 152
learning style, discovering your 50
lectures, getting the most out of 50–51
Lei, Vivien 121–122
Li, Christina 106–107
Liang, Alan 154–155
LinkedIn 63
—building your profile on 64–67
—importance of email contacts on 57
listening
—gaining insight through 28
—leadership and 210–211

micromanaging 191
mistakes
—avoiding future 21
—calmness in dealing with 21–22
—fixing 21
—judging others' 22
—keeping in perspective 22
—learning from 19, 20–21, 23
—resilience and 20
—taking responsibility for 19, 20

names, skills for remembering 110–112
negative feedback, using to improve 8
negatives, turning into positives 2
negotiation see also influence
—the power of authenticity in 124–125
networking 56
—authenticity in 59
—business cards and 58
—exploring existing contacts 56–57
—in-person events and 57
—LinkedIn and 57
—listening and 59
—making an impression in 59–60
—nervousness and 58
new workplaces, building rapport in 92–93

office politics 105
opportunities, taking advantage of 142–145
organisational skills
—developing your 136–138
—importance of 135
—leadership and 136

Parr, Ash 68–69
perseverance
—goals and 16
—in jobs 152, 173
Phegan, Ashleigh 40–41
Pitcher, Tim 113
popularity 6
Prasad, Rimal 163–165

Prasad, Shane 32–33
prioritising 135, 180–183
procrastination 38–39
promotions 179–180
public speaking, building self-confidence through 39

rapport
—building in a new workplace 92–93
—building with your boss 102
—building with your colleagues 102–105
recommendations on LinkedIn 66–67
rejection, dealing with 163, 198
respect
—for others 28
—importance of 6
—in teamwork 116, 118, 121
—influence and 125–126
résumés
—addressing key selection criteria in 73
—cliches, avoiding in your 74
—contact details on 75
—cover letter for 75
—creating an effective 72–76
—introduction in your 72
—length of 73
—proofreading your 75
Roche, Demara 25
Ross, Olivia 146–147

saying 'no' 159–162
—in different contexts 157–159
self-awareness
—developing 6–7
—journaling and 10
—leadership and 211
self-criticism 8
Singh, Kevin 88–89
Smith, Liam 184–185
stress, dealing with 8
study
—creating an environment for 50
—importance of finishing your course of 154
—planning your 50
—selecting your course of 47–48, 49
—taking advantage of opportunities in 51–52
—the four themes of success in 47–49
—time management in 50, 53
success
—celebrating 17, 52
—in the workplace 93

Taskunas, Patrick 61–62
teams
—good personality mixes in 45
—improving underperforming 117–120
—working in underperforming 116

uniqueness, harnessing your
8–9
universe, creating your own
43–45

volunteering
—gaining experience
through 25, 32, 51
—LinkedIn and 65
—to do unpopular jobs 153

Walker, Chad 11–12
work–life balance, myth of
203–204 *see also* work–life
quality
work–life quality, achieving
204–206

THE NAKED CEO

Visit thenakedceo.com to continue the conversation online.

The Naked CEO Alex Malley, chief executive of CPA Australia and host of the Nine Network Australia's *The Bottom Line*, invites students and professionals to join him as he reveals the truth about how to build a big life.

With Alex as your mentor and adviser, thenakedceo.com provides a 24/7, 365 day-a-year access-all-areas pass to global leaders and brands, advice to help secure graduate opportunities and vital information about how to develop the skills that could launch your career into the stratosphere.

By visiting the website, you can:

- ask your mentor Alex a question and receive a personal video answer

- explore practical job-seeking and career-building advice

- gain skills and insights that will give you an unfair career advantage so you can get in, and get ahead, in your dream job, and have a big life.

> The Naked CEO website offers practical, real-life examples for how to best take our skills to market, and this you can't find anywhere else.
>
> —The Naked CEO student guest, Demara Roche

From suspended schoolboy to disruptive CEO, Alex always does what he believes in.

Follow Alex on Twitter: @AlexMalleyCEO

Learn more with practical advice from our experts